D0845761

Advance praise for
by Joe Mysak

"Joe Mysak has written **the new bible for municipal-bond issuers**. The search is over; this book **provides clear guidance and smart answers** for everyone in the field."

> JAMES B. G. HEARTY
> Managing Director
> Lehman Brothers

"Joe Mysak explains even the most complex subjects with a refreshing simplicity. He maintains his ever-present skepticism about much of what usually turns out to be flimflam in the guise of new products and financial engineering. **This is a book for anyone**, even investors without specialized financial backgrounds, **who needs to understand what all the noise is about in a bond sale**."

> FRANK R. HOADLEY
> Capital Finance Director
> State of Wisconsin

"Joe Mysak has prepared a "pocket-sized financial adviser" for both large and small municipal-bond issuers. The book provides **a good mix of timeless as well as currently topical subjects**. All recently elected **public finance officials should read this book**."

> CHRISTIAN McCARTHY
> Managing Director, Municipal Markets
> Merrill Lynch & Co.

"The *Handbook for Muni-Bond Issuers* is what public finance professionals want to have on their shelves, both **a good read and a useful reference**. Joe Mysak treats the fundamentals—and the foibles—of the municipal bond market in **clear, concise language** and takes time to tour some frequently bypassed, but very practical subjects, like winning bond elections and investing bond proceeds."

> JOHN PETERSEN
> President
> Government Finance Group

"Joe Mysak has once again proven that he's **the conscience of the public finance business**."

> F. JOHN WHITE
> Chief Executive Officer
> Public Financial Management

"Joe Mysak's book will guide any municipal finance professional through the labyrinth of bond issuance. His **user-friendly style** bypasses the usual esoteric and technical jargon. **Finally, a book of practical solutions for any muni-bond issuer**."

> ED ALTER
> Utah State Treasurer

JOE MYSAK

HANDBOOK FOR
MUNI-BOND
ISSUERS

JOE MYSAK

HANDBOOK FOR
MUNI-BOND
ISSUERS

FOREWORD BY MICHAEL R. BLOOMBERG

BLOOMBERG PRESS

PRINCETON

Books are available for bulk purchases at special discounts. Special editions or book excerpts can also be created to specifications. For information, please write: Special Markets Department, Bloomberg Press.

This publication contains the author's opinions and is designed to provide accurate and authoritative information. It is sold with the understanding that the author, publisher, and Bloomberg L.P. are not engaged in rendering legal, accounting, investment-planning, or other professional advice. The reader should seek the services of a qualified professional for such advice; the author, publisher, and Bloomberg L.P. cannot be held responsible for any loss incurred as a result of specific investments or planning decisions made by the reader.

First edition published 1998
1 3 5 7 9 10 8 6 4 2

Mysak, Joe

    Handbook for muni-bond issuers / Joe Mysak.

      p.   cm. -- (Bloomberg professional library)

    Includes index.

    ISBN 1-57660-023-8 (alk. paper)

    1. Municipal bonds.   I. Title.   II. Series.

    HG4726.M95   1998

    332.63'233- -dc21   97-52168

                                                CIP

Acquired and edited by Steve Gittelson and Jacqueline Murphy

Graphs and charts by Myra Klockenbrink

Book design by Don Morris Design

For Jim Grant,

and no wonder.

— J.M.

CONTENTS

Acknowledgments

THE WRITER THOMAS WOLFE once wrote a story called *Only the Dead Know Brooklyn*. The title was an allusion to the sheer size of the borough, which before its inclusion into the City of New York at the turn of the century was once one of the biggest cities in America.

In similar fashion, we have the municipal bond market, which is vast, and which is particular and specific to a remarkable degree. No one can know the entire municipal market. This book is an attempt to distill 16 years of experience in covering this most fascinating of all credit markets into a brief and readable format. I have had a lot of help along the way.

First, I wish to thank James Grant and Jay Diamond at *Grant's*, who in 1994 welcomed me into their publishing family. *Grant's Municipal Bond Observer*, a fortnightly magazine aimed at the trade, was born. In 1997, they further endorsed the idea of launching a special magazine aimed at municipal bond issuers: *Grant's Municipal Bond Issuer*. It was not until I put together a fortnightly magazine that I really became a student of the market. Jim and Jay are thorough professionals dedicated to putting out first-rate products, and are also good guys.

There are not many municipal bond journalists, but I have had a chance to work with the best ones, including John Allan, Bill Ryan, Craig Ferris, and John McCorry. These were my teachers.

And then there are my colleagues, the former merry band who comprised the staff of what we then termed the Greatest, Most Elite Newsgathering Organization in the History of the World, now sadly dispersed. These include Jack Doran, Steve Dickson, Dennis Walters, Lynn Stevens Hume, Vicky Stamas, Karen Pierog, April Hattori, Keith DuBay, Sean Monsarrat, Patrick Fitzgibbons, Jim Murphy, Ted Hampton, Aarons Pressman and Task, Kathie O'Donnell, David Gillen, Sharon King, Suzanne Montanaro, Susan Kelly, Christina Pretto, Rob Taylor, Maggie Soares, and Joan Pryde. These people made it a lot of fun to come to work in the morning.

This book would not have been possible without the active assistance of professionals in the field: Jim Hearty, Gary Killian, and Spencer Wright of Lehman Brothers; Christian McCarthy of Merrill Lynch; Jim Lebenthal; Doug Watson and Fran Laserson of Moody's; Vlad Stadnyk of Standard & Poor's; Byron Klapper and Frank Rizzo of Fitch Investors Service; Austin Tobin of Delphis Hanover; Mike Ballinger of MBIA; J.B. Kurish of the Municipal Issuers Research and Analysis Center; Sylvan Feldstein; and Jack Kraft of the American College of Bond Counsel.

Not a few issuers have helped me over the course of the years, including Utah's Ed Alter, Frank Hoadley of Wisconsin, Jan Rzewnicki of Delaware, Bob Lenna of Maine, and Joe Lhota and Mike Geffrard of the City of New York. Three former bankers, Mike Lissack, Steve Strauss, and Bill Wood, helped me on the reinvestment of proceeds and yield-burning sections.

Special thanks, too, to Steve Gittelson of Bloomberg Press—who during a party at Janet Sullivan's asked, "Do you want to write a book for us?"—and to my editor at Bloomberg, Jacqueline Murphy.

The glossary is largely drawn from the book I wrote with George J. Marlin in 1992, *The Guidebook to Municipal Bonds*, which was published by *The Bond Buyer*. The book is not only out of print, but also out of date, which goes to show how fast things have changed in the municipal market.

Finally, I would like to thank some friends for their support over the years, including the aforementioned Marlin, Patrick Foye, Mike Crofton, Mark Reed, Parker Bagley, and Steve Gustavson. And finally I would like to thank my wife, Susan Merett, who is also my best friend.

FOREWORD

BY MICHAEL R. BLOOMBERG

SOME YEARS BACK, *The Bonfire of the Vanities* author Tom Wolfe suggested to Joe Mysak that he write a book about the municipal bond market. Call it *The Dark Continent,* Wolfe suggested. You hold in your hands the result.

The municipal market is a vast place, and not a little scary for those not privy to its mysteries. Despite its intimate connections with all of us—look no further than the sewers and the sidewalks beneath your feet for examples of things financed through the sale of municipal bonds—the municipal market has never really become a part of our financial culture.

The consequence is that most people probably know more about how to sell an initial public offering in the stock market than they do about selling municipal bonds. How do you choose a financial adviser, an underwriter, a bond counsel? How are bonds priced? How do underwriting syndicates work? Why do we need a credit rating? How do we pay all these people? This book takes you through the whole process, step by step.

The municipal market is, by any measure, big. It has been estimated that more than 80,000 entities have the authority to issue municipal debt. And every year, more than 7,000 of them do so, selling some 10,000 separate bond issues. As Joe Mysak points out, the municipal market is particular and specific to a remarkable degree. But there is a basic framework to all municipal bond transactions, and it is explained here.

That basic framework now includes heightened regulatory scrutiny. The Securities and Exchange Commission Office of Municipal Securities's advice to issuers is simple and direct: You are responsible for your bond issues. You can rely upon the professionals you hire, but only up to a point. You have to understand exactly what is going on and why. Before you can do this, you have to know what questions to ask.

I believe Joe Mysak delivers solid advice on how to tap a market that has become a wonder of the (increasingly decentralized) world. I think you will find this book a reliable source of guidance and good practice.

A Few Notes on the Format

◆ This book packs a lot of information. It is designed to be functional as well as factual, trim enough to be carried in a coat pocket and taken on the road, and read easily on train, ship, or plane.

◆ The book's organization accommodates your hectic schedule. The material flows logically and offers real-world applications at every turn.

◆ Graphics are designed with the busy reader in mind, highlighting important concepts from the experts in color throughout.

Michael R. Bloomberg

INTRODUCTION

ALL MUNICIPAL FINANCE officers have the same goal when they determine that the time has come to tap the municipal bond market—borrow money at the lowest cost, legally. Most officials seldom use the municipal market and find it unfamiliar turf when they do venture onto it.

This book will help municipal bond

issuers realize their goal, by providing an understanding of how the process of public finance works, who the cast of characters attendant to a sale are, how the regulators see the market, how others have used innovations in their bond sales, how to measure bond performance using simple benchmarks, and how to work with underwriters should they choose negotiated sale.

The easiest way to understand municipal bond sales is to look at some successes and failures.

◆ The City of Richmond, Virginia designed a variable-rate, short-term note program that allows it to borrow for temporary capital and operating needs. "This program will enable the city to sell bonds more infrequently and in larger amounts, which is expected to lower debt issuance and debt service costs," Moody's Investors Service noted approvingly.

Lesson: *Concentrate on lower debt service costs (see Chapter 2).*

◆ Utah, one of only six states rated triple-A by all three of the major rating agencies, instituted a program that allows the state's 40 school districts to use the state's rating as a guarantee on their own debt, thus giving them the chance to save millions of dollars on their borrowings.

Lesson: *Only half the states have these kinds of guarantee programs. If your state does, it can dramatically lower yields on your borrowings (see Chapter 12).*

◆ San Francisco, mindful of one rating agency's dictum that it "is more expensive to lure a new franchise than to retain an existing one," used bond insurance to get voters to approve $100 million in bonds for a new stadium for the city's 49ers National Football League (NFL) franchise. The agreement with the insurance company provided that the insurer, not the city, would make up any shortfalls in the special tax revenues that pay debt service. Usually bond insurance covers debt service only if the issuer actually defaults. "The upset victory confounded polls that showed the measure trailing by as much as 23 percentage points," according to the Bloomberg wire service.

Lesson: *Bond issues on ballots need champions (see Chapter 9).*

◆ Constrained by certain aspects of the Tax Reform Act of 1986, New York City was forced to sell taxable bonds, rather than tax-exempt bonds. The city found that in some instances it could sell such bonds more cheaply abroad than at home, and it set up a special agency to sell yen-denominated bonds in Japan. The city later estimated that interest rate savings on one bond issue approached nearly $4 million.

Lesson: *Your job is to borrow money at the lowest cost, legally (see Chapter 2).*

To be sure, these are examples of advanced municipal finance strategies. But they show just what you can accomplish if you devote some time and attention to the municipal market.

Unfortunately, however, you are bound to learn more lasting lessons from the market's horror stories. Cautionary tales abound. Here are some specific problems to avoid:

◆ Brevard County, Florida commissioners

approved the construction of a new admin-istration building using non–voter-approved securities called certificates of participation, whose repayment was subject to annual appropriation. Critics of the building forced a referendum on whether to repay or repudiate the issue.

Lesson: *Don't assume your project with a nonessential purpose has popular support.*

◆ Lewisburg, Tennessee sold some securi-ties to build a golf course. It took longer to build the golf course than first estimated, and revenues fell short. The city chose not to appropriate money to cover debt service payments, an option clearly outlined on page 9 of the official statement. The trustee sued the city, and it took more than a year of legal wrangling to refinance the debt.

◆ Lake Elsinore, California built a new baseball stadium for its minor league team. Cost overruns forced the city to borrow more to complete it. At the same time, the city embarked on an ambitious economic development program, eventually borrowing more than $8,000 for every man, woman, and child in town. Almost all of the debt was backed by appropriations, which the city, to its credit, tried to make. The city now faces a costly series of debt refinancings.

Lesson: *Don't assume such a thing as no-fault public finance actually exists.* Economic development projects begun with the best of intentions, and financed by securities backed solely by revenues from the project itself, may nevertheless wind up devouring your time, money, and credit.

◆ The City of Vallejo, California sold securities to build the Marine World/Africa USA theme park, which was run by a non-profit educational foundation. The city kept pouring money into the project in an effort to increase attendance, and eventually it decided to take over the theme park itself. The city is now trying to sell it.

Lesson: *To be successful, theme parks need major new attractions every two years.* Major new attractions require big money.

◆ Two Mississippi counties, Hinds and Warren, sold a series of housing bonds for which more than 5 percent of the proceeds were used to pay issuance costs. Internal Revenue Service (IRS) rules limit cost of issuance to 2 percent. The IRS determined that the bonds were taxable. The counties had to enter a closing agreement in which participants in the deal paid $1.2 million to the IRS.

Lesson: *Don't break IRS rules governing bond issuance.*

◆ Maricopa County, Arizona was charged by the Securities and Exchange Commission (SEC) with securities fraud for selling two general obligation bond issues totaling almost $50 million without disclosing that the county's finances were deteriorating. The county agreed to a cease and desist order.

Lesson: *Don't break SEC rules on disclosure of material events.*

◆ One of the nation's largest municipal authorities, the Washington Suburban Sanitary District, with an excellent record of administration and operation, nevertheless got into trouble with both the SEC and the

IRS when it allowed its financial adviser to handle setting up escrow accounts for a refunding bond issue. The district may have to pay the IRS more than $4 million in "deflected arbitrage" as a result of the two agencies' investigations into a practice known as "yield-burning."

Lesson: *To avoid self-dealing and conflict of interest, have each professional working on your transaction handle only one job.*

◆ Bondholders are suing the City of Denver for not clearly disclosing in the official statements to its borrowings for a new airport that a state-of-the-art automated baggage system might not work as designed.

The faulty baggage system delayed the opening of the airport and depressed the bond prices.

Lesson: *Disclose all material information in your official statement.*

THESE EXAMPLES SIMPLY demonstrate that it pays to do it all right in the first place. The new regulatory reality in the municipal market is that the IRS is examining more bond issues to ensure that they comply with tax law, and will declare issues it determines in violation to be taxable, unless the issuer pays a penalty. The SEC is equally serious in its pursuit of issuers, as well as their professionals, who violate securities fraud laws. The message from these regulatory agencies is simple and clear: *You, not the professionals you hire to help you, are responsible for your bond issues.*

This need not be terrifying. Done the right way, your bond issue is nothing less than a glory of the credit markets and a wonder of the world. Municipalities from London to St. Petersburg are eagerly studying how thousands of U.S. municipalities each year are able to borrow money cheaply and efficiently owing entirely to their own credit. But done the wrong way, the costs that result from lost or impaired market access, decline in credit rating, and legal maneuvering are almost incalculable.

The process of coming to market, as we shall see, resembles less the streamlined workings of an assembly line than it does a walk down a long corridor, with stops at appropriate offices along the way. Surprisingly enough, the inhabitants of these offices do not all know one another, even by name. These professionals are usually tightly focused on a single subject, such as bond law in a single state, tax law, or how to run the numbers on an advance refunding to discover if it makes sense.

Over the years, municipal bond issuance

has become, not more national in scope, not more consistent and uniform, but actually more specific and particular. In New Jersey, for instance, school districts that sell certificates of participation are ineligible to receive state aid for debt service payments; only bond issues qualify for such aid. In Wisconsin, not only out-of-state bonds are subject to taxation, but so are most in-state bonds.

There are hundreds, if not thousands, of such peculiarities on the books.

The most important thing for you to remember about the professionals who will help you come to market in the new era of increased regulatory oversight may be summed up in three unhappy words: Trust no one. It is no longer enough—if indeed it ever was—for issuers to hire professional help and then to rely on it. You must become deeply involved with every step of a financing, and you must understand precisely what is going on. Now let's take a look at the basics.

CHAPTER 1

GETTING STARTED

MOST MUNICIPAL FINANCE officers have more in common with the director of finance whom I once called at home—only to be told that he was at work in the cranberry bog and would call me back later—than they do with Wisconsin's full-time director of capital finance, or New York City's comptroller.

Unlike these professionals, who have access not only to all of the analytical tools described later in this book, but also to professional staffs, most municipal finance officers find bond sales to be a very small (but irksome) part of the job. They represent a knotty problem that must be handled once every few years. With this in mind, let's review the market basics.

First of all, there is no one thing called the "municipal market." Those who generalize about such a thing (as in, "Hey, what about all these scandals roiling the municipal bond market?") are unlikely to know what they are talking about.

The municipal market is an over-the-counter market, meaning that there is no organized central exchange where a bell goes off to signal the start and finish of the day's trading. Buyers and sellers communicate and negotiate by telephone. If an investor and a broker agree on a transaction at midnight, that is the "municipal market" at that point in time.

Comparatively few of the millions of separate bonds outstanding, totaling more than $1.3 trillion at last count, actually trade at all. And more often than not, the prices of inactive securities are based on little more than a very educated guess.

What is a **municipal bond**? In simplest terms, it is an interest-bearing certificate issued by a government when it wants to borrow money. Most of today's market is electronic, and comparatively few investors ever get to see the single representative paper "bond" held at a repository. A bond is a loan, unlike a share of stock, which represents ownership in a corporation. Stockholders agree to ride out both good times and bad, including bankruptcy. Bondholders agree to loan money in return for interest and return of principal. This is why bonds are considered one of the most conservative investments.

Municipal bonds are singular and highly specific. The various characteristics that set each of them apart are far more numerous than the qualities they share. One analyst for a portfolio manager recently observed that there were more than 50 varieties of municipal bond for him to study, and that was just a rough estimate.

The "municipal market" is highly fractured. Municipal market? There are highly evolved state-specific markets (California, Colorado, Florida, Illinois, New York, Texas); regional markets (the upper Midwest, the Deep South); and sector markets (health and hospital bonds, housing bonds, public power bonds, American Indian tribe financings, even high-yield bonds).

Most of the market is state specific. In other words, a Florida municipal bond firm might spend all its time dealing strictly with the issuers and buyers in its own state. It is not too far off the mark to say that, because of their independent, decentralized nature, nearly every state has a highly developed municipal bond market all its own. Comparatively few firms operate on a truly national basis. Those that do (the major Wall Street firms), typically deal with only the largest bond issues and issuers.

Most municipal bonds are relatively small. In 1996, more than $183 billion in municipal bonds were sold, but in more than 11,500 issues: The average size was approximately $15 million. And even this number is skewed higher by a relative handful of blockbuster deals. About 85 percent of the bonds sold each year are for an average of just over $5 million.

But the 80–20 rule also applies to municipal bond issuance: 80 percent of the actual number of bonds sold make up only about 20 percent of the dollar volume. These larger, more lucrative deals are the bond issues that Wall Street finds it worthwhile to chase. But in reality, small issuers just like yourself make up the bulk of the business. It is up to you to insist on the same level of service the larger issuers get in the big market.

Why do you sell bonds? For the same reasons that individuals take out loans. You, your municipality, does not have ready money at hand; or you find it more efficient to match up liabilities with the useful life of whatever it is you are paying for; or you think that a project's users should also pay for it; or any one of a number of reasons.

Municipalities—and the term covers everything from a fire district, to an authority, on up to a state—today sell bonds for purposes ranging from repairing roads and bridges, to paying for sewer systems and mass transportation systems and even telecommunications systems, to funding pension liabilities, to building theme parks and sports stadiums and acquiring historic properties, to preserving farmland and beaches.

In a typical week, the municipal market handles 194 separate bond sales; the number rises to 250 or more in busy times and falls to 150 or less in a holiday-shortened week. In a typical week last year, as the York County, Pennsylvania Solid Waste and Refuse Authority was preparing to sell $114 million to refund bonds it had sold at higher interest rates back in 1985, Fergus Falls, Minnesota sold $6.6 million in general obligation bonds to fund various public improvements, and the Darlington, South Carolina School District sold $3.1 million to pay for school improvements.

Municipalities also sell bonds to help spur economic activity. What could be more of a public purpose than providing jobs, a North Carolina politician asked not too long ago, in response to criticism about a bond sale for a factory.

What indeed? But the most important question buyers of your municipal bonds have is this: How will they be repaid? Normally, economic development bonds are repaid either by special assessments or from the revenues a particular project generates. But what happens if not enough people move into a new housing development, and the special assessments they pay just do not cover debt service? What happens if not enough people visit a new aquarium? Are the bonds insured? Did the municipality make any promises to step in if those revenues proved insufficient?

The answer has a direct impact on how much you will have to pay to borrow money from investors, which leads us to a discussion of the kinds of municipal bonds that are sold.

In this discussion, **bond sale** refers to the original pricing and sale of your bonds: the primary market. **Secondary market** refers to the trading of bonds that have already been sold. Some bonds trading in the secondary market date from the 1950s and 1960s.

Municipal Bond Types:
GO Bonds and Revenue Bonds

THERE ARE TWO main categories of municipal bonds: general obligation (GO) bonds and revenue bonds. There are of course some hybrids, but in order to understand all else that follows, you must understand the distinction between these two.

General obligation bonds are backed by the full-faith and credit pledge of an issuer with taxing power. Most historians agree that New York sold the first GO bonds in the United States, in 1812. The Municipal Securities Rulemaking Board's (MSRB) *Glossary of Municipal Bond Terms* (this handy 117-page paperback guide has not been updated since 1985, but it remains a valuable resource, should be on the desk of every issuer, and is available from the MSRB for the bargain price of $1.50; 202-223-9347) defines GO bonds:

> Such bonds constitute debts of the issuer and normally require approval by election prior to issuance. In the event of default, the holders of general obligation bonds have the right to compel a tax levy or legislative appropriation, by mandamus or injunction, in order to satisfy the issuer's obligation on the defaulted bonds.

Characteristics of GO Bonds versus Revenue Bonds

GO Bonds

◆ Backed by full-faith and credit taxing power of municipality.
◆ Typically must be approved by voters.
◆ Provides cheapest rate of financing.
◆ Citizens' "willingness to pay" difficult to quantify.
◆ Vulnerable to property tax revolts.
◆ Very conservative structure.

Revenue Bonds

◆ Backed by identified revenues, usually user fees.
◆ Need not be approved by voters.
◆ Rates usually 25 to 55 basis points higher than GO rates.
◆ Relies solely on "ability to pay."
◆ Invulnerable to property tax revolts.
◆ Very flexible in structure.

The GO bond is the most basic type of municipal bond. From an investor's point of view, it is also the safest, which is why GO interest rates are typically cheaper than those on revenue bonds by anywhere from 25 to 50 basis points or more (bond yields are figured in basis points, which are one-hundredth of a point; GOs, then, are typically one-quarter to one-half point cheaper for you to sell than revenue bonds). It is no mystery why. In essence, you are telling your lenders that you will do whatever is necessary, that you will raise taxes to whatever level is required, in order to pay the debt service or annual principal and interest payments due on your bonds.

Who sells GO bonds? Any municipality with the power to levy taxes: New York City sells GO bonds, hundreds of millions of them every year. So does the State of California. But so does the First Colony Municipal Utility District #2 in Texas, which in October 1997 sold $2,170,000 in general obligation bonds.

The other kind of municipal bond, called a **revenue bond**, is secured by a specific revenue stream such as tolls or other user fees. The concept of using a particular project's fees to support it dates from approximately 1885. In 1931, the Port of New York Authority, as it was then styled, added a new spin with its consolidated revenue bond, which allowed for the revenues from a number of different projects undertaken by the same agency to back the bonds sold to build those projects. This enabled stronger projects, whose revenues exceeded expectations, to support weaker ones, whose income might not cover their own costs for decades.

A more modern example of a revenue bond was the $20 million issue sold by Iredell County, North Carolina for the Iredell Memorial Hospital in the fall of 1997. The bonds are, in the words of the official statement, "payable solely from, and secured solely by a pledge of, the Net Revenues" of the hospital.

Or take the University of North Carolina at Chapel Hill. In 1997 it sold several million dollars in "Student Fee Bonds," which are backed by a special $10.25 per-student, per-semester fee. The university's Board of Governors promises that it will:

> Fix, charge and collect from each student . . . the Student Indebtedness Fee and that from time to time and as often as it is necessary it will adjust the Student Indebtedness Fee so that the Revenues will at all times be sufficient to equal 120 percent

of the average annual Principal and Interest Requirements on all the Student Fee Bonds then outstanding. . . .

GO and revenue bonds are not the only kinds of bonds sold. Municipalities also sell bonds backed by the so-called moral obligation of the issuer to make up shortfalls in debt service. And they also sell securities called **certificates of participation**, which are backed by nothing more than a promise by the issuer that it will appropriate money annually to pay debt service. Analyst Robert Zipf defines these in his *How Municipal Bonds Work:* "A certificate of participation is a security that represents an interest in payments which the issuer has promised to make, but which are subject to annual appropriation by the issuer's governing body. The issuer must actually appropriate the funds each year."

Until the 1970s, the issuance of GO debt far outstripped sales of any other kind. Since then, however, the tide has turned the other way, and now 70 percent or so of the dollar volume of bonds sold every year is in revenue bonds.

Why the sea change? For one thing, a municipality's tax base is limited, which is why the adjective precious is so often used to describe GO bonding capacity. For another, revenue bonds generally are not subject to the whims of voters, which may at times seem downright capricious. For a third, the idea that actual users, rather than all taxpayers, pay for a project is intrinsically attractive in a democracy. Finally, during this period there was a boom in public finance generally, with municipalities rushing to foster economic development projects of all kinds.

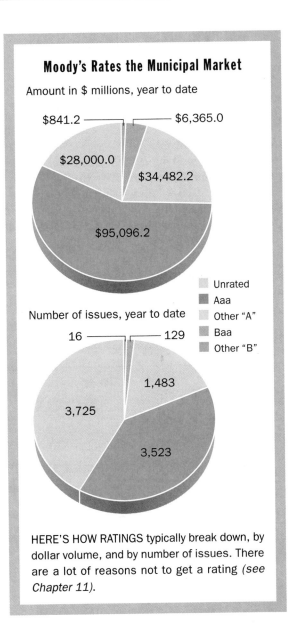

Moody's Rates the Municipal Market

Amount in $ millions, year to date

$841.2 — $6,365.0
$28,000.0
$34,482.2
$95,096.2

Number of issues, year to date

16 — 129
1,483
3,725
3,523

Legend:
- Unrated
- Aaa
- Other "A"
- Baa
- Other "B"

HERE'S HOW RATINGS typically break down, by dollar volume, and by number of issues. There are a lot of reasons not to get a rating *(see Chapter 11)*.

Revenue Bonds and Authorities

REVENUE BONDS ARE more often than not sold by special municipal entities known as authorities, created either to build particular projects, such as airports or bridges or golf courses, or to act as conduit agencies for sales of so-called industrial development bonds that benefit private companies.

Perhaps the most famous of the authorities was the first, the aforementioned Port of New York Authority, founded in 1921. According to Julius Henry Cohen, the first general counsel of the agency, it was modeled on the Port of London Authority, which in turn got its name from an act of Parliament. "Nearly every paragraph [of the act] began with the words 'Author-

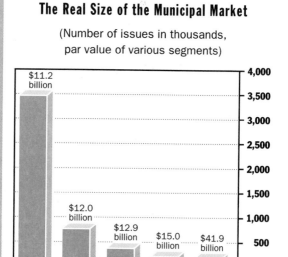

The Real Size of the Municipal Market

(Number of issues in thousands,
par value of various segments)

$11.2 billion — $10 million and under

$12.0 billion — $10 million-$25 million

$12.9 billion — $25 million-$50 million

$15.0 billion — $50 million-$100 million

$41.9 billion — Over $100 million

ity is hereby given.' So Lloyd George said, 'Let's call it the Port of London Authority,'" wrote Cohen in his 1946 memoir, adding, "If London could prosper with an Authority, New York could do well with one." There are thousands of municipal authorities in operation today.

The boom in revenue bonds and independent authorities has been accompanied by some criticism. Not too long ago, for example, *Boston* magazine carried a cover story called "The Shadow Government," which typified the resentment the independent authority structure had engendered. The magazine described the more than 500 authorities that had mushroomed across the commonwealth of Massachusetts: "It is an invisible government that functions with

WE HERE PRESENT the real municipal bond market, a very different market from the one in which Wall Street is interested. Of the more than 5,020 issues sold in 1997, 69 percent were in the $10 million-and-under category, while those under $25 million accounted for almost 85 percent of total municipal bond issuance.

The $23 billion in par value contained in that almost 85 percent of the number of issues accounted for only 25 percent of all actual dollar volume sold, which was $93 billion. The average size of a bond issue has increased slightly from the recent historical norm, to $18.5 million from around $15 million. But the average size of the deal in the 85 percent of the market described above is a little more than $5 million. The municipal market is overwhelmingly regional in both origin and appeal.

SOURCE: SECURITIES DATA CO.

little oversight by elected officials—except, of course, the fortunate few who regard certain authorities as their personal fiefdoms," the article began. "No matter how well authorities serve their functions, there are too many of them now, and too many more are being created every year. What's more, they are borrowing too much money and making too many decisions on the public's behalf out of the public's sight and beyond the public's control."

Municipal Market

(Number of issues and par value, weekly)

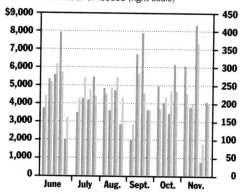

THIS CHART ILLUSTRATES the dollar volume and number of issues sold from June through October 1997. In a given week, 194 separate transactions can be expected to come to market. A busy week can mean 250 or more deals; a light week, about 150.

And as recently as 1997, Indiana State Treasurer Joyce Brinkman came out and asked her own state's lawmakers to stop creating new authorities: "What alarms me most is that no one can tell you how much debt the state has because it is so fragmented among these little debt kingdoms."

Despite this criticism, and much more like it, it seems unlikely that authorities will be reined in significantly any time soon. They are a fact of life and simply too useful to abandon.

The Cast of Characters

BEFORE WE GET to the ways municipal bonds are sold, following is a brief description of the cast of characters, in their usual order of appearance:

Financial adviser (FA). Helps you decide if a bond sale is appropriate at all; then assists in its planning and preparation.

Bond counsel. Opines on the legality of the issue and its tax exemption or taxability. Often an excellent source of ideas on the structure of the deal.

Underwriters counsel. A lawyer involved in the transaction, who represents the securities firm buying your bonds. Some municipalities find it in their interest to hire special disclosure counsel to help them with matters relating to ongoing disclosure after the sale.

Banker. Specialist in public finance at a bank or brokerage house. Helps with the actual structuring and marketing of the bond issue.

Analysts. Some work for rating agencies and assess your bond issue for a credit rating. Some work for insurers, who determine if they want to insure your issue. Some work for underwriting firms and provide detailed research reports on your credit to the sales staff and other clients of the firm. Finally, some work for the so-called buy-side or institutional investors such as mutual funds or insurance companies, where they study your bond issue to decide if they want to buy it.

Underwriter. Professional at a bank or brokerage house who buys your bonds in order for the firm's sales force to resell them to both institutional and retail investors. Occasionally, firms operate alone, but they usually run in packs, termed underwriting syndicates.

Paying agent. Responsible for paying principal and interest, when due.

Trustee. Represents the bondholders; usually also represents the paying agent.

Broker's broker. A broker who handles blocks of securities in the interdealer market.

Evaluator. An analyst who works for an interdealer broker, a "broker's broker," who determines prices on bonds trading in the secondary market.

CHOOSING YOUR METHOD OF SALE

The Great Debate:
Competitive versus Negotiated Sales

ONCE YOU MAKE the decision to sell bonds, you must next decide how to sell them. There are two chief ways: through **negotiation** with a preselected team of underwriters, or via a **competitive sale** featuring sealed bids. The competitive sale versus negotiated sale debate has been one of the most divisive in the market's history.

Although these are the leading methods of sale, other methods exist—subscription, modified auction, direct sales to retail, private placement. But they are far less prevalent and are used only in certain special situations. For most of the 20th century, almost all issuers sold bonds competitively, or, as some old-timers refer to it, by "advertised sale." It remains popular today, especially for smaller and comparatively simple, straight vanilla bond offerings. You advertise the bonds for sale and list the date, time, and place where sealed bids will be taken. The bids are then opened and evaluated. The bonds are awarded to the underwriter providing a bid resulting in the lowest true interest cost or net interest cost.

You do not necessarily have to award the bonds at all, if you are dissatisfied with the number or quality of bids—underwriters sometimes make mistakes in bids. Although not exactly common practice, it is not unheard of. On the other hand, there are also rare occasions when issuers receive no bids at all and must reschedule the sale or determine to come to market in some other fashion. Why might a bond issuer not receive a bid? Generally speaking, when underwriters think there is something not quite cricket going on. This happened in 1997, when a couple of New Jersey school districts tried to use their power of eminent domain to condemn their own schools, and thus trigger an optional and extraordinary provision to call some outstanding debt at par.

The districts figured that they could have saved $2 million by doing so. But underwriters figured that the school districts were using a legal fiction (the schools were just fine) that would result in bondholders being hurt (and, consequently, filing lawsuits). They figured that this was a way for issuers to invoke, in essence, par calls at their own discretion. So they didn't bid on the securities.

Issuers walk a fine line between coming up with new and creative ways of saving money (or, as more often happens, having bankers and financial advisers who pore over their bond documents looking for new and

Competitive versus Negotiated Bond Sales

Competitive

◆ Removes politics from the picture.

◆ More risky for underwriters: "Bonds are bought, then sold."

◆ An all-or-nothing proposition. You accept the best bid, or not.

◆ Best for relatively simple, straightforward credits.

◆ Easiest to sell.

Negotiated

◆ Often very politicized.

◆ Less risky for underwriters: "Bonds are sold, then bought."

◆ You negotiate with the underwriter for the best price.

◆ Best for complicated, "story" credits, first-time issuers.

◆ Requires adequate preparation, timely information flow.

creative ways for issuers to save money) and thereby alienating not only their current bondholders, but also buyers at future bond sales. The controversies surrounding this area in recent years have revolved chiefly around the question of whether or not issuers have the right to call bonds away from bondholders earlier than the bondholders had been promised. If an investor owns a bond trading at 110 and believes that it is going to mature in six years more, that investor is understandably not very happy when you want to call his or her bond now, at 101.

But let's return to negotiated sale. The rise of public,

independent "authorities" and the special-purpose revenue bond neatly coincided with increased use of negotiated sale, which overtook competitive sale as the main means by which thousands of issuers sold their bonds in the mid-1970s. By the 1990s, more than 80 percent of the dollar volume of bond sales was being done through negotiation, and some observers predicted that it would not be too long before competitive sale was a relic of the past. (Once again, remember to differentiate between the dollar volume of the market and the actual number of issues in the market).

Competitive sale never became extinct. In fact, competitive sale subsequently rebounded smartly, to about 30 percent of dollar volume. Why the turnaround? Simply put, competitive sale survived because what everyone had been saying for years about negotiated financing—that there was the potential for political, regulatory, and financial abuse—was true.

What brought the matter to a head were two well-publicized cases, one concerning the New Jersey Turnpike Authority and the other the State of Louisiana, where a number of Wall Street firms claimed that they had been shaken down for cash by shell companies run by political operatives who apparently brought little to the actual structuring, sales, and marketing of a deal besides those political connections. New Jersey responded by prohibiting negotiated underwriting on all but a few transactions.

The ratio of negotiated to competitive deals, on a dollar volume basis, is currently running about 3:1. On an actual number-of-issues basis, the ratio is closer to 3:2.

This ratio will probably remain intact for the foreseeable future, primarily because negotiated sale offers you flexibility in pricing and offers buyers ease of access at a cost—at least at this writing—barely above what you might expect to pay in a regular competitive sale. Indeed, negotiated sale in certain cases might even be a better "buy" for you as an issuer than competitive sale, so long as you remember to retain a certain probing skepticism about the process, to ask the right questions, and to ensure that the selection of the professionals involved is itself as competitive as possible. Remember, your goal is to sell debt at the lowest interest cost you can get, legally. If a negotiated sale enables you to do this, then you would be wise to use negotiated sale.

Negotiated sale was not always as relatively inexpensive as it is today. Intense competition and increased efficiency among underwriters has made it so. Why negotiated sale was, and should be, more expensive is a matter of logic: A custom-made suit costs more than one purchased off the rack. This is why for much of the municipal market's history, negotiated deals were much more expensive, at least in terms of underwriter compensation, than competitive transactions.

There were and are good reasons to choose the negotiated route on a bond sale. But they do not, in the main, apply to what we think of as "most" issues and issuers, which are rather small, and usually uncomplicated.

How then can we account for the incredible penetration of negotiated sale? It was the result of a concentrated, aggressive, and almost unrelenting campaign by bankers, who in essence extended their argument from "We can sell complex issues for you" to "We have such a powerhouse sales force that we can sell literally any issue for you and save you money, besides."

There happens to be a lot of truth to the argument. On a negotiated sale, the buyers—in other words, the underwriters—are guaranteed an investor market for the bonds, because in fact they have most or all of them already presold. They can get you very good prices on your bonds. On the other hand, they can also deliver what amounts to sweetheart deals to their buyers. Unless you have a real feel for the market and for the process, you can wind up paying too much and not even know it.

On the actual day of the pricing, the senior manager of the deal usually winds up doing little more than allocating the money earned by the various underwriters for selling their portions of your bond issue. On a competitive deal, as F. John White of Public Financial Management, a financial advisory firm, has noted, "you're never 100 percent sure" about whether buyers will materialize at the levels where your bonds are priced. As one critic described it, the modern negotiated syndicate enables underwriters to avoid risk almost entirely—which, he hastened to add, was not part of the definition of *underwriting,* but rather of an agent or middleman.

There are three times when you should definitely choose the negotiated method of sale for your bonds:

1 When you are going to sell a large issue—not just objectively "large," like a $700 million deal, but large relative to what you have sold in the past. If you usually sell $10 million deals and decide the time is right for a $30 million issue, you might well choose the negotiated route.

2 When your issue is complex, or unusual, or has a story behind it that must be explained to buyers in some depth.

3 When the market itself is deteriorating. There are times when the bond market can be characterized as weak or nervous or sloppy. Simply put, this is when buyers feel that interest rates are headed higher. Who wants to buy a bond that pays 5 percent, when, if you were to wait a week or a month, you could buy one that pays 5.25 percent or 5.50 percent?

In general, you would do well to remember the advice of one bond buyer, a portfolio manager at a large trust company. There are generally two times when "complex" or "creative" structures are used, he said. One is when an issuer does not have, for one reason or another, easy access to the market. The other is when bankers are looking to make more money.

Politics Enters the Picture

BANKERS MAY HAVE pushed negotiated sale, but they did not find issuers unreceptive to their pitch. Negotiated sale, for one thing, gives you a real hand in the deal by allowing you to choose the members of your underwriting syndicate. This can thoroughly politicize the underwriting process. Needless to say, politics has nothing to do with getting the lowest interest rate on your bonds.

If there was a great deal of money to be made in public finance, certain issuers in the 1980s decided they wanted to be part of the way it was doled out, thus transforming the sale of bonds from fairly straightforward transactions designed to raise capital, to yet another way of dispensing patronage to their friends, certain full-voiced political constituents, or (in the days before the MSRB, which oversees the municipal market, issued its Rule G-37, forbidding campaign contributions by bankers) to especially generous municipal bond underwriters.

Political cynics might dismiss this criticism with, "Well, it's always been that way." But the facts prove otherwise: In the municipal bond market, at least, it was not always this way. At a competitive sale, the bonds go to the best bidder in the market, according to pure mathematical calculation. Period. Politics, cronyism, and personal agenda—such as a future job at an investment banking firm—do not enter into it. This is why competitive sale is the best and safest all-around method of sale for issuers to use.

Why Are So Many Deals Negotiated?

HOW, IN 1990, did 73 percent of credits rated double-A and triple-A, including state general obligations (precisely those credits the market hungers for most), come to be sold through negotiation? Markets are, after all, supposed to reward better credits with easy and inexpensive market access. George Friedlander, director of high-net-worth portfolio management at Smith Barney, which is one of the top underwriters of municipal bonds, analyzed the situation in 1991. He wrote that negotiated sale allowed bankers to structure a deal to minimize the effective interest cost of the issue, using techniques "that simply cannot be used on a competitive deal," including presale marketing, adjusting the structure of an issue, and adjusting the size—even on the day of the sale, and even as the deal was being priced. He also noted,

> Negotiated financings are sold and then bought, while competitive issues are bought and then sold. In other words, effective pre-sale marketing, and the ability to "fine-tune" the price of an issue after initial pricing, can allow an issue to be placed, in large part, prior to being sold to the underwriters. On a competitive issue, on the other hand, a large proportion of the bonds may have to be sold before the bid is submitted. In other words, competitive underwriting often entails far more market risk for the underwriters—and a "risk premium" often will show up in the yield, rather than in the gross spread.

In addition, Friedlander observed that the rise in negotiated transactions speeded up in the early 1980s, when the household component of municipal bond investors increased in importance. Retail sales, the analyst said, generally require the type of presale marketing that can be provided only through negotiation. "Retail account executives, and underwriting firms, cannot afford to do extensive marketing for an issue that they may only have one chance in five, or one in 10, of buying at competitive sale," according to Friedlander, who is one of the more astute observers of the market.

What accounted for the rise of the negotiated sale? For one thing, more complex financings. For another, more new issuers in general, and more revenue bonds in particular. For a third, the politicization of the market. Finally, very aggressive sale of the technique by bankers.

In a 1962 booklet entitled *Preparing a Bond Offering of a Local Government for the Market,* the editors of *The Daily Bond Buyer,* as it was then styled, observed, "Since it is so generally recognized that a negotiated deal opens the door for serious abuses, there is a possibility that the fear of criticism may cause public officials to shy away from this form of sale in certain instances where it could be used to advantage." This was written, incidentally, when negotiated sale made up less than 10 percent of the market and annual volume totaled less than $10 billion.

As the Government Finance Officers Association (GFOA) put it in 1984, in a booklet entitled *An Elected Official's Guide to Government Finance:* "Competitive sale should be used to market debt whenever feasible." Issuers should ensure that underwriting profits are reasonable and that the costs to the public are minimized.

A decade later, the onus had shifted from, "The underwriters may make too much money" back to, "You as an issuer are going to cost your municipality too much money because you're taking your eye off the ball, and worrying about things that don't really matter in bond issuance." In the 1994 *Debt Issuance and Management: A Guide for Smaller Governments* (also published by the GFOA), author James C.

Joseph noted, "One of the most common concerns about the negotiated sale process is that the underwriters may be chosen for reasons other than their ability to effectively structure and market the bonds. Such reasons include everything from friendship with the issuer's staff to political favoritism resulting from campaign contributions."

Even *The New York Times* editorialized in 1993, "Commonly, a government or public agency chooses a financial firm to underwrite the sale of a bond issue, then negotiates terms—rather than awarding the business on the basis of competitive sealed bids. That practically invites abuse and scandals, and too often the underwriters gain their entree with generous campaign contributions or, worse, kickbacks."

The paper observed of the negotiated versus competitive argument, "There is no conclusive evidence that either way always works better. But evidence abounds that sealed bidding helps to neutralize the stench of political influence." This is strong stuff, coming from the newspaper of record.

There is nothing intrinsically wrong with the negotiated method of sale. The real key to thinking about how to come to market is flexibility. Governments should use both methods of sale. The government that always uses negotiated sale, that uses the same underwriting team year after year, that embarks on new capital programs without putting the work out for bid in the form of requests for proposals (RFPs), that rigs RFP results by choosing a fifth-ranked firm over the firm that won the beauty contest that is the RFP process—all this will raise, or should raise, a red flag in the eyes of civic activists, of reporters, and of the citizenry in general, that the public finance process is not working as it should. These abuses of the process can end up costing your municipality big money in the long run.

Public Financial Management's F. John White observes:

> Governments should familiarize themselves with the mechanics of the market and evaluate the potential benefits of each approach before making a decision. In the final analysis, however, the marketing of municipal bonds is not an exact science and there is no way to determine with certainty that one method of sale is better or worse than another for a particular issue.
>
> I think issuers should do both. I think if you're a well-known issuer who sells regularly, even if you primarily sell your deals negotiated for whatever reason, every now and then you should sell a deal competitively, just to test the market. You're the Massachusetts Water Resources Authority, there's no reason you can't do a simple, $40 million, competitive deal and just benchmark how everything is doing. We did a deal, I think it was Michigan, where they did a competitive deal in the morning and a negotiated one in the afternoon. And if you won the competitive deal, you also got the negotiated one, which was more complex. I think the real small stuff—the bank-eligible, under-$10-million-in-size issues—should go competitive.

◆ In March 1994, the State of Michigan, which had not competitively bid any state transportation debt for a decade, offered underwriters the chance to bid on a $150 million Michigan State Trunk Line new-money bond issue, with the understanding that the winner of the competitive deal would also be named the senior manager of a negotiated refunding deal that would be sold within 15 days. Nick Khouri, then the state's chief deputy treasurer, said, "We want to get an aggressive interest rate on the competitive deal and on the refunder."

They did. Nine syndicates bid on the deal, with a mere 6.5 basis points separating the low and high bids. The winning bid produced an interest cost of 5.75688 percent—almost 10 basis points better than the state had wanted when it started.

Subscription Sale

NEITHER FISH NOR FOWL is the subscription sale. The City of Lewisville, Texas was the first issuer in modern memory to use this method of sale, put forward by First Southwest, the largest financial adviser in Texas.

"The director of finance at the time for the city, Connie Maxwell, disliked all the hype associated with choosing an underwriter for her bonds," recalled W. Boyd London, Jr., of First Southwest. "We proposed the subscription method to her for two refunding transactions totaling $34 million. She liked the concept of increasing her exposure to the investor through the use of multiple investment bankers and the inherent sense of fair play involved in awarding business to those that prove that they can sell bonds."

In a competitive sale, you ask underwriters to bid. In a negotiated sale, you choose your underwriter beforehand and help establish the price of your bonds. In a **subscription sale**, you invite underwriters to sign up to sell whichever of your bonds they wish to sell.

The Lewisville sale worked as follows: The city and First Southwest invited between 50 and 60 underwriters to participate in the transaction. Those underwriters who chose to participate sent back signed subscription forms.

First Southwest ran the sale much like the senior manager would, initially pricing the bonds, establishing the takedown, or sales commission, and taking orders. The firm did not purchase or sell any bonds itself, but it did have a standby agreement to take bonds any underwriter failed to pay for at delivery.

"We identified three reasons to recommend the transaction to Lewisville," London continued. "First, we felt that there was an opportunity to reduce total underwriting expenses by utilizing this method. We thought that those savings would initially total $0.50 to $0.75 per thousand. In fact, when the smoke cleared we had saved approximately $36,000 in underwriting expenses and had identified another $17,000 that could be saved on the next transaction through future reductions in underwriters counsel expense. This was not accomplished by reducing takedowns, as seems to be the norm these days. We saved in the expense component and the management fee. In total, the city achieved $1.05 average reduction in total underwriting costs. Taking advantage of future savings on underwriters' counsel, most issuers on a $34 million issue could save $1.55 or so per thousand.

"Second, the marketing and allocation method employed spread Lewisville's bonds among more underwriters, effectively expanding the city's market. On two $34 million transactions, we had 26 underwriters submit orders. We felt this would stimulate future demand for the City's bonds. We think that this in fact has proven to be the case.

"Finally, it gave all underwriters an equal chance at participating in the transaction, including minority and regional firms. Those underwriters who were able to perform were rewarded, and those who could not received nothing. As you are aware, in most underwriting transactions, the senior manager monopolizes the majority of the business. This has only worsened in recent years. This concept really leveled the playing field and maximized incentive."

London called the subscription sale "not appropriate for all credits and markets. It can be used effectively by good market names in good markets." He said, "It should be viewed as simply another tool in the box to be used in those situations where it works best."

Don't Run afoul of Regulators

WASHINGTON IS WATCHING. The SEC is charged with protecting investors in your bonds and cares a lot about how you present them.

◆ In 1989, the cities of Wasco and Avenal in southern California used some of the proceeds of so-called Marks-Roos bond issues (a type native to the California market and designed to increase economic development) to buy some Mello-Roos bonds sold by Nevada County, which is 250 miles away, in northern California. First California Capital Markets was the underwriter of the Wasco and Avenal bond pools, the underwriter of the Nevada County bonds, and also the financial adviser to Avenal and Wasco on their bond pool investments.

The Nevada County bonds went into default in 1993. The SEC investigated and eventually sent letters to a dozen parties to the transaction, including Nevada County, announcing that it intended to prosecute them for fraud or recklessness in bond disclosure. Mounting a full defense is estimated to cost $1 million or more, money that Nevada County is ill-prepared to spend. Avenal and Wasco have to live with defaulted bonds in their portfolios.

◆ William Baker, assistant director of the SEC Division of Enforcement, tells bond lawyers that issuers must disclose in their official statements if a bond issue might be declared taxable. "If you are taking a fairly aggressive tax stance and you are aware that there is a danger the IRS might view it differently, that could give rise to a disclosure issue and it may be something that investors are entitled to know before they invest in the bonds," he says.

The preceding examples all occurred within the past three years, and they represent just how the federal government has increased its regulation, surveillance, and enforcement in the municipal market. Baker told me in 1997 that he thought the municipal market seemed to work very well "with a minimum of oversight," and added that most of the problems he had seen had been "at the fringes"—in other words, between small dealer firms and small, infrequent issuers.

Asked to elaborate on what kinds of things the SEC is looking at, Paul Maco, head of the SEC Office of Municipal Securities, said that areas include disclosure problems, conflicts of interest, and yield-burning, which we discuss in Chapter 6. He reiterated Baker's observation that there was nothing to suggest that the market has "problems that go to its core," but it seems that the wild and woolly days when reporters could write about the "largely unregulated" municipal market are clearly over.

How to Choose Your Debt Sales Team

WHETHER YOU USE negotiated or competitive sale, you are going to need a team to help with the financing. The most important single act for you to undertake is the choice of competent professionals. As the IRS and the SEC have made abundantly clear, simply hiring good help is not enough. But it does get you a good deal of the way.

An unwatched transaction is a dangerous one. For the bond sale process to work best, you have to put together a team that is responsive to your concerns. The team must work in cooperation, but it also works as a system of checks and balances.

The two most important members of the financing team are the bond counsel and the financial adviser (FA). The bond counsel, in essence, rules on whether or not the bond issue is (a) legal and (b) tax-exempt. The FA helps you to keep track of everyone in the transaction, provides you with a detailed road map of how the bond sale will proceed, and helps with the selection of the other participants. The FA also helps run the numbers. The process can easily take six months or more, depending on the type of bonds being sold, and it may even take years in the case of a new municipal entity selling its first bond issue.

The members of the financing team should be selected by a competitive RFP process, in which the firms are asked to provide their professional qualifications in a written document that can run anywhere from 6 or 7 pages to 20 or more. For the widest possible distribution, an advertisement notifying the industry that an RFP is available can be published in *The Wall Street Journal* or in *The Bond Buyer*. Some issuers simply send out the RFP to a limited number of firms. Advertising, however, works best and is the favored method.

The municipality then evaluates each candidate, invites selected ones for oral interviews, and makes its choice. This is usually done by assigning the various finalists a value and then choosing the one who comes in first. It is not unheard-of for a firm to be chosen for a top spot despite not coming in first, and the reason is usually political favoritism. Frankly speaking, choosing the seventh-ranked firm for the job will look awfully fishy to reporters who bother to use the Freedom of Information Act to find out about the process.

The GFOA gave the best advice to its members about the process in *Debt Issuance and Management: A Guide for Smaller Governments,* by James C. Joseph, a 136-page paperback published in 1994. "Be as flexible as possible in determining whether or not a proposal meets the requirements of the RFP; the issuer's objective is to identify the firm best qualified to assist with the financing, not to test their ability to respond to RFPs."

Two divergent and disturbing trends have lately developed in how issuers choose the professionals involved in their bond sales. On one hand, certain issuers have decided that bond sales work best when attended by multiple professionals—co-bond counsel, co-underwriters counsel, co-financial advisers, special brackets of underwriters. These issuers seem to think that bond sales are the proper places to reward constituents and interest groups. They festoon a bond sale with extraneous numbers of professionals, all of whom add a lot to the cost of issuance and usually very little to the actual efficiency of the sale.

Playing politics with municipal finance is nothing new, of course, but it is being scrutinized at the federal and state levels, and issuers have to weigh whether or not the game is worth the candle, as the expression goes. There is little difference between the city that put three co-bond counsel, two co-underwriters' counsel, and two co-financial advisers on a single bond issue, and got away with it, and the city that tacked on a local underwriter who, some Wall Street underwriters alleged, "did no work" but got paid. This last matter sparked a state investigation of the matter in Louisiana, by the way, with all the attendant legal costs and newspaper headlines.

It is not a smart matter of public policy to engage in such white-collar patronage games. It is distracting, a waste of taxpayers' dollars, time-consuming, and unfair to the other professionals who bring their expertise to the transaction. It is also dangerous: An amateur's mistake could cause an issue to unravel and be declared taxable now or several years from now. What happens after that? The usual welter of lawsuits, investigations, claims and counterclaims, and bad publicity. Is it really worth it?

Certain issuers, on the other hand, have taken a different but no less extreme route, in deciding that all services should be awarded strictly on the basis of price. Although in the short term this may provide issuers with low-cost services, in the long run it could promote some real problems. If you refuse to compensate your financial professionals adequately, sooner or later those financial professionals will dedicate fewer resources to your business. Ultimately, the business will go to cut-rate firms that are inadequate or incompetent. You get what you pay for.

Select professionals on the basis of their expertise and qualifications for the job, not on politics or price. Now let's get our financial adviser.

GETTING
ADVICE

THE MOST IMPORTANT professional involved in the transaction, and one with whom you will presumably set up a long-term relationship, is the financial adviser. The financial adviser will help you navigate through the bond sale, regardless of whether you sell bonds competitively or through negotiation.

A good financial adviser, or FA for short, steers you clear of trouble and is with you at the end of the sale. A bad FA is one who has his or her own agenda, or whose pay is entirely contingent on a bond sale taking place. A good FA will advise you when a bond sale is inappropriate, or when some other course of action will serve your needs better. Yet FAs happen to be a relatively recent addition to the cast of characters at a bond sale. Before the 1980s, few issuers used them, usually instead relying entirely on their bond lawyers. Today, few smart issuers do without FAs, and for the very good reason that the market is more complicated than ever before, and full of shoals for the unwary.

THE LATE LENNOX MOAK, in *Municipal Bonds: Planning, Sale, and Administration* (1982), wrote that the financial adviser helps the issuer in at least 11 ways:

1 Making a presentation to rating agencies.
2 Helping to calculate the timing of a bond sale.
3 Determining the range of interest costs for different alternative potential means of financing.
4 Determining the reasonableness of fees for other specialized services.
5 Providing an idea of what underwriters' fees should be.
6 Deciding on call provisions suitable for the bond issue.
7 Sizing and structuring the bond issue.
8 Setting bidding requirements and other terms of public sale, *or*
9 Helping to conduct a negotiated sale.
10 Evaluating the sale when it is finished.
11 Evaluating the performance of each of the members of the syndicate in a negotiated financing.

Moak compiled this list in 1982; as you might imagine, today it could be expanded to include such things as assisting on reinvestment of proceeds, determining the advisability of entering into a swap transaction, and deciding how to put together your debt service reserve fund, to name a few.

As you can see, these are highly specialized jobs that affect every aspect of your bond sale. The importance of selecting an expert, qualified FA who can assist you on each of these jobs and more—such as helping to set up the competitive process to select a paying agent, trustee, and even printer—is paramount.

FAs come in two distinct varieties: **financial advisers who are also members of large underwriting firms**, such as Merrill Lynch and Goldman, Sachs, Smith Barney, and Lehman Brothers; and so-called **independent financial advisers**, who work for firms such as Public Financial Management, Public Resources Advisory Group, and Government Finance Group. "Independent" FAs do not trade, underwrite, or sell bonds.

There has been some conflict between the two in recent years, with the independents contending that only they can be totally objective because they work on only one portion of a transaction. They point to instances where financial advisers have also insisted on providing reinvestment services, or where banks have tied FA services to the provision of a letter of credit to issuers. The other side has said that only financial advisers with trading and underwriting desks can have a real feel for the market. Today, there are more independents in the top-10 ranks of financial advisers than there are firms that also underwrite and sell bonds.

In the end, you should choose your FA based on expertise. The crucial point is that your FA should be working for you alone and not be allowed to handle any other job. This is the only way to guard against potential conflicts of interest and be sure that you are getting the best advice for your money.

The FA is in your corner from the very beginning of a deal, and usually has a long-term relationship with you that extends well beyond a single transaction. It is not that unusual to contract with an FA, for example, for a two- or three-year engagement, and have that person work on all aspects of your capital financing plans.

You depend on your FA for independent, objective

advice. What you have to guard against are FAs who have side agreements with other firms that compensate them for specifically recommending their services.

The whole business of side agreements and fee-sharing was at the heart of the *United States v. Mark S. Ferber* fraud trial, which took place during the summer of 1996.

Ferber began his career in 1980 at Kidder, Peabody & Co., and rose swiftly in the industry, putting together a large and loyal following of issuer clients for his financial advisory services. At the height of his powers, he was known as a municipal bond power broker in Massachusetts. His downfall came when a secret arrangement he made with Merrill Lynch & Co., to market their swaps to his clients in return for an annual retainer, was uncovered by the Massachusetts Inspector General's Office. Ferber was found guilty of fraud and subsequently sentenced to 33 months in a federal prison for, in essence, not disclosing to his clients, clearly and in writing, the private agreement he had with Merrill Lynch. Federal prosecutors deemed that the public was "deprived of its right to honest services."

How to Choose a Financial Adviser: Look Before You Leap

IN EARLY 1997, the GFOA released a "recommended practice" for issuers preparing RFPs for financial advisers and underwriters. The document contained points clearly designed in response to the allegations of abuse, corruption, and conflict of interest in the municipal market.

The GFOA recommends that you use an "open, merit-based process" when selecting the members of your financing team, and that an RFP process "serves that purpose. It promotes fairness and objectivity; allows the issuer to compare qualifications, ideas, and prices of respondents; and helps the issuer to obtain the best price and level of service."

The GFOA continues, "Issuers should have a clear understanding of their needs, both short- and long-term, and determine whether services are needed on a transaction-specific or on-going basis. Ongoing contracts with financial advisers or relationships with underwriters should be reviewed periodically to ensure that issuer objectives continue to be met."

As far as fees, the GFOA states: "Fees paid to financial advisers should be on an hourly or retainer basis reflecting the nature of the services to the issuer. They should not be contingent on the sale of bonds to remove the potential incentive for the financial adviser to recommend the issuance of bonds."

The GFOA also advises that issuers examine prospective firms with particular vigilance in regard to spotting "any finder's fees, fee splitting, or other contractual arrangements of the firm that could present a real or perceived conflict of interest, as well as any pending investigation of the firm or enforcement or disciplinary actions taken within the past three years by the SEC or other regulatory bodies."

In addition, "Issuers may also want to include a provision in the RFP restricting any firm from engaging in activities on behalf of the issuer that produces a direct or indirect financial gain for the firm, other than the agreed-upon compensation, without the issuer's informed consent."

SAMPLE RFP

Here is what the City of New York asked on its RFP for financial advisory services in 1994:

1 Please describe, in detail, the **scope of services** that your firm has provided for at least three clients

that you believe are relevant in preparing your firm for the role of financial adviser to the City of New York.

2 Competitive vs. Negotiated Sales: Please provide your firm's criteria for determining the appropriateness of the competitive or negotiated methods of sale for any given borrowing.

3 Competitive Sales: Assuming that the City issued debt through a competitive sale, please give your recommendations on the specific steps to be taken in order to effect the sale. How would you solicit bids? Specifically, how would you solicit bids from institutional and retail firms, regional specialty firms, minority-owned and women-owned firms and small and New York City firms? How, if at all possible, might derivatives be incorporated into a competitive sale?

4 Size of the City's Management Group and Financings:

a) What does your firm recommend as the optimal size and structure of a negotiated underwriting team for the City's general obligation bond program? What is your opinion about rotations of senior and/or co-managers? Address the role of institutional and retail firms, regional firms, minority-owned and women-owned firms and small and New York City based firms.

b) Assuming an annual capital program of $2.4–$2.7 billion for the upcoming fiscal years, what would your firm recommend as the optimal size of individual City financings and the frequency of such financings a year? Please evaluate the trade-off between these two variables.

5 Relations with Rating Agencies, Investors and Credit Providers:

a) Rating Agencies: What specific strategies or recommendations does your firm have to improve the City's relations with rating agencies? In the last three years, have you helped a client improve its credit rating? If so, please describe your effort to do so and the actual rating change. What would you propose that the City do to improve its debt rating?

b) Investors: What specific strategies or recommendations does your firm have to improve the City's relations with investors? What specific actions do you recommend to the City to ensure the optimal marketing and placement of its debt to both institutional and retail investors?

c) Credit Providers: What specific strategies or recommendations does your firm have to improve the City's relations with credit providers? [This question refers to bond insurers and banks that provide letters of credit to support variable-rate debt programs.]

6 Evaluation of Derivative Products: How would your firm suggest we evaluate the use of derivatives and their benefits in future financings? What qualitative and quantitative methodologies would you employ? What access does your firm have to current market information on the sales and trading of derivatives of New York City securities?

7 Refunding and Tender Offers:

a) What analytical criteria would your firm employ to evaluate refunding opportunities?

b) How would your firm structure and use a tender offer as an alternative to a traditional advance or current refunding?

8 Pricing: How would your firm provide timely, accurate and detailed market information necessary to ensure that the City achieves the best market price on its negotiated underwritings? What market information can you provide to the City at a pricing session?

9 Quantitative Analysis: Please describe your firm's quantitative capabilities and how you would organize your firm to 'run the numbers' for New York City. Please perform a break-even analysis with respect to the use of capital appreciation bonds as a portion of a New York City serial bond structure.

10 Taxable Debt: Please discuss the products and markets to either lower borrowing costs or diversify the sources of capital for the City's taxable bond program.

11 Underwriter Performance: What techniques would your firm suggest to evaluate senior and co-manager performance on any given City financing? What sources of information would you utilize?

12 Fees: Please provide a proposed fee arrangement and structure for your firm's financial advisory services.

13 Firm Information/Equal Employment Opportunity:

a) How many persons are employed by your firm in professional and non-professional, or support, categories or titles? How many of such employees work primarily in financial advisory services?

b) Does your firm qualify as a women-owned or minority-owned business as defined by regulations of the City of New York?

c) Describe your firm's equal employment opportunity policies and programs.

d) Identify all adverse determinations against your firm, or its employees or persons acting on its behalf, with respect to actions, proceedings, claims or complaints concerning violations of Federal, State, or City equal employment opportunity laws or regulations.

e) Complete the attached employment statistic forms for your firm's public finance and municipal sales and trading professionals.

YOUR CITY MAY NOT be considering a multibillion-dollar capital program like New York's, but it is clear that the RFP can provide you with a plentiful supply of specifics about both the firm competing for the financial advisory (or bond counsel, or underwriting) slot, and the financing process. In fact, reading past responses to RFPs, which should be on file, can be a real education.

Your professionals help you to sell bonds and raise capital. The main job is still yours, however, and that job is to "sell" the municipality. Chapter 4 describes the right way to do it.

HOW TO SELL
BONDS
THE RIGHT WAY

Full Disclosure

THE "OFFICIAL STATEMENT" is as close as many bond buyers will ever get to the issuer, and it is important for the OS, as it is known for short, to be as comprehensive as possible. The OS functions as an offering prospectus and lays out what the bond proceeds will be used for, how the bonds will be repaid, and what the financial condition of the issuer is.

They may look like collections of so much legal boilerplate, but official statements are a crucial part of the financing process. They were once fairly skimpy documents, but events such as the New York

What Your Official Statement Should Contain

1 Cover page, showing amount, maturities, interest rate, price; or yield, ratings, tax opinion, and underwriting syndicate (if negotiated).

2 Introductory description.

3 Plan of financing.

4 Sources and uses of funds. This is a table showing how much money is being raised through the bond issue and where it is going, including underwriter's discount and costs of issuance.

5 Description of the bonds. This includes redemption provisions.

6 Information on the system of book entry only. Usually furnished by the Depository Trust Co., this explains how the electronic book-entry system works and why bond buyers no longer receive engraved bond certificates.

City financial crisis of 1975 and the Washington Public Power Supply System bond default of 1987 helped fuel the trend of providing the investor with more and better information. In addition, today underwriters must review the OS before they sell bonds to investors. Whether or not those actual documents would have made a big difference had they been bigger or stuffed with more information is a matter for debate. The SEC requirement that issuers disclose more information, and more regularly, is not a matter for debate.

Consider, for example, a recent State of Hawaii general obligation bond issue. The OS contained information on the authority and purpose of the bond issue, security for the bonds, as well as general and financial information. It also included the latest audited financial statements. Under "general infor-

7 Security and sources of payment for the bonds.

8 Summary of certain provisions of the resolution.

9 Tax-exemption.

10 Legal matters.

11 Ratings.

12 Continuing disclosure resolution. This is where the issuer promises to provide information vendors with updated financials, notice of material events, and the like.

13 Underwriting (if negotiated). The underwriters agree to purchase the bonds at a certain price, less the underwriters' discount.

14 Financial adviser.

A number of appendices usually follow this basic information, containing the latest financials, form of bond counsel opinion, insurance policy, if any, and other miscellaneous information.

mation" was included everything from the details of its outstanding debt, to its tax structure, to the outlook for its economy. There was even a section about a state program to set aside public land "for the rehabilitation of native Hawaiians," called Hawaiian Home Lands.

All of this material is designed to give potential buyers a snapshot of the issuer and to highlight any sources of anxiety. Hawaii was selling a general obligation bond, perhaps the simplest credit there is, and yet its OS still amounted to well over 100 pages. More complicated credits can run to hundreds more.

Not only must you fully disclose your municipality's financial situation, you must also promise to continue providing the market with information as it is available. You are expected to file annual reports as well as updates on material events, the same as any corporate borrower—not to the SEC but to a **nationally recognized municipal securities information repository**, or **NRMSIR**. NRMSIRs have been set up by Bloomberg, Standard & Poor's, *The Bond Buyer*, Moody's, and the Municipal Securities Rulemaking Board (MSRB), among others.

According to the SEC, "there is a general consensus among participants in the municipal securities market that investors need information about the following events, among others, where material." Here, then, are the SEC's so-called **11 Deadly Sins**—material events that must be disclosed to investors as soon as possible after they occur:

1 Principal and interest payment delinquencies.
2 Nonpayment-related defaults.
3 Unscheduled draws on reserves.
4 Unscheduled draws on credit enhancements.
5 Substitution of credit or liquidity providers, or their failure to perform.
6 Adverse tax opinions or events affecting the tax-exempt status of the security.
7 Modifications to rights of security holders.
8 Bond calls.
9 Defeasances.
10 Matters affecting collateral.
11 Rating changes.

IN 1996, THE National League of Cities; the National Association of Counties; the National Association of State Auditors, Comptrollers, and Treasurers; and the Government Finance Officers Association (GFOA), in consultation with the SEC, put together an eight-page booklet entitled *Questions to Ask Before You Approve a Bond Issue.*

The groups printed 40,000 copies of the booklet, but such was the hunger by municipalities for information on the disclosure process, that within a month, they had to go back to press and print more. The booklet introduction notes that it was designed "to assist state and local issuers in ensuring that their bond disclosure documents comply with federal securities laws. It includes questions that are intended to produce disclosure documents that meet the needs of a reasonable investor purchasing a jurisdiction's bonds or notes."

The booklet contains three sets of questions issuers should ask themselves about their own bond issues. The first are below; the other two sets of questions are contained in the sidebar on pages 70–72.

◆ Why are the bonds being issued?
◆ What is the purpose of the issue and how will the bond proceeds be used?
◆ What type of bonds are being issued?
◆ How will the bonds be repaid?
◆ Are there circumstances that might interfere with repayment?
◆ What is our financial condition and what circumstances might cause it to change?
◆ What options do bondholders have if revenues are not sufficient to pay them?

THESE ARE ALL GOOD, general questions that rely primarily on common sense. The GFOA, the National Association of Bond Lawyers, the Bond Market Association, and the National Federation of Municipal Analysts, among other groups, are all just dying to supply you with more specifics about what to disclose. In addition, associations of issuers just like you have put together similar guidelines.

For example, the Association of Local Housing Finance Agencies has specific suggestions for housing bond issuers; the National Council of Health Facilities Finance Authorities has guidelines for health and hospital bond issuers. Housing and health and hospital

Questions Officials Should Ask Themselves and Their Staff Members

1 How have we allocated responsibilities for the preparation of the official statement? Have we clearly defined the responsibilities of all participants in the transaction?

2 What processes or procedures have been established to select qualified professionals? How are we relying on them, and is our reliance appropriate? How are they compensated?

3 What have we done to establish the accuracy of financial and operating information and its disclosure in the official statement (OS)? Has anything happened since the date of the financial statements that needs to be disclosed?

4 What policies and procedures have we developed to determine whether material conflicts of interest exist that need to be disclosed?

5 What procedures have we established to accurately describe the project, the bond terms, the sources of repayment, and the risks associated with the project? What procedures have we established for the investment and disbursement of the bond proceeds?

6 Do our procedures permit the underwriters to carry out their "due diligence" and other responsibilities?

7 Have we fully considered any questions asked by the rating agencies?

8 What continuing disclosure responsibilities have we assumed, and what procedures have we established to meet them? Who will determine and file the annual financial and material event disclo-

sure information? Have we designated an individual to speak to the market on our behalf?

9 If we are relying on the bond counsel, financial adviser (FA), or trustee to evaluate and meet our continuing disclosure requirements, what procedures are in place to keep them apprised of our financial condition and other material information?

10 Have our procedures produced an official statement that we feel accurately presents our financial condition and discloses the information a reasonable investor needs to know? Have all the right people reviewed it?

Questions They Should Ask Outside Professionals

1 What is the nature or scope of the written opinion or certification, if any, that you are giving in this transaction and relating to the disclosure document? Have we given you access to the information you need?

2 Have you explained to us all aspects of the structure or nature of this transaction so that you are confident we fully understand all critical aspects? Does our official statement adequately address any concerns you have about this transaction that a reasonable investor would consider important?

3 Are there any matters regarding your participation in this transaction about which you should have made us aware, including potential conflicts of interest?

4 Has your review of the relevant financial documents and other materials, including the official statement, raised any concerns regarding this

(continued on following page)

borrowing? Do these concerns need to be disclosed?

5 Are you aware of any circumstances in which we, our staff, or others have not complied with our procedures so that we can ensure that our official statement adequately and accurately describes this transaction?

bonds are some of the most complicated in the market, chiefly because, in the case of the former, they carry a wider range of call options than are generally used by municipalities, and in the case of the latter, because of the nature of their cash flows and the consolidation in the industry.

As mentioned in Chapter 1, the municipal market is vast, and particular and specific to an amazing degree. The more information you can gather about the types of bonds you are going to sell, and what you say about them, the better an issuer you will be.

You are responsible for your bond issue. In the wake of the Orange County, California bankruptcy, the SEC released a report, which said in part,

Public entities that issue securities are primarily liable for the content of their disclosure documents and are subject to proscriptions under the federal securities laws against false and misleading information in their disclosure documents. In addition to the governmental entity issuing municipal securities, public officials of the issuer who have ultimate authority to approve the issuance of securities and related disclosure documents have responsibility under the federal securities laws as well. In authorizing the issuance of securities and related disclosure documents, a public official may not authorize disclosure that the official knows to be false; nor may a public official authorize disclosure while recklessly disregarding facts that indicate that there is risk that the disclosure may be misleading.

In other words, the price of bond-issuing authority is eternal vigilance.

Legal Advertising

DISCLOSURE OF A different kind is contained in legal advertising. In addition to advertising RFPs for services, municipalities must take out legal ads on at least three other occasions. The first is a **notice of sale**, in the case of a competitively bid financing. The second is a **notice of call**, or of full or partial redemption. The last is a **notice of default**.

As with almost everything else in the municipal market, the legal requirements for each of the kinds of advertising are state specific, and sometimes even municipality specific. Notice of sale advertising is certainly recommended for all competitive bond sales, although, as Frank Hoadley, the capital finance director of Wisconsin, says, "All you have to do is get on the calendars" of underwriters. More than one state has allowed its issuers to run "summary notices of sale," which cuts down on the size and cost of legal advertising.

Most bonds now are sold book entry, registered, and immobilized in a single location, usually the Depository Trust Co. The process is largely electronic, and issuers know precisely who their bondholders are and can notify them if and when they intend to redeem their securities. This was not always the case. Bonds were once engraved documents, and owners clipped the coupons and brought them to a bank for their interest payments.

The notice of redemption or notice of call advertisement is a relic of this time, and it is part of the covenant established between the bond buyer and the bond issuer. It also functions, however, as insurance for the issuer. If a bond is called, and a bondholder somehow does not learn about it—and so loses months or even years of interest—he nevertheless has no legal standing to sue the issuer, provided that the issuer has advertised the call, usually in a local paper, and in one of national circulation, such as *The Bond Buyer* or *The Wall Street Journal.* The trustee for the bonds is usually responsible for the placement of these ads, which service is included in their fees.

It is worth noting that some issuers have become so concerned with what and how information relating to their financial condition and bond transactions is disclosed that they have retained special disclosure counsel. Edsell M. Eady Jr., of the law firm Musick, Peeler & Garrett, discussed this subject in the Fall 1996 issue of *The Urban Lawyer.* Eady observed:

> It is vital for the issuer to define, and for counsel to acknowledge, the distinct professional responsibilities of such [bond] counsel to the issuer on the adequacy of disclosure. Traditionally, bond counsel is engaged by or on behalf of the municipal securities issuer to prepare operative transaction documents rather than disclosure, and to act impartially and objectively in rendering its legal opinions about the validity, security, and tax-exemption of a municipal issue. In this respect, bond counsel's role is inconsistent with the more familiar role of legal counsel as advocate for a client's interests.

He concluded: "In the heat of an SEC enforcement action, the adequacy of disclosure is certain to be the subject of advocacy as well as objectivity. Accordingly, an issuer's reliance-on-counsel defense will be optimized where disclosure counsel independent of bond counsel has been engaged directly by the issuer." And so another lawyer is brought to the party. In the age of increased SEC scrutiny, it may prove to be a very wise investment. It is well to remember that finance officers are not judged by how cheaply they manage to bring a bond issue to market.

Paying the Lowest Interest Cost

INFORMATION IS YOUR FRIEND when it comes to getting the lowest cost financing. Fortunately, today a wealth of information is available about municipal finance in general, and bond yields in particular, if you know where to look.

The easiest way for you to discover what kinds of yields investors are demanding for bonds similar to yours is to look at the various yield curves available in the market. A **yield curve** simply shows you a number representing an interest rate for each year, from 1 year out to 30 and in some cases 40 years. When plotted on a graph these numbers produce a curved line.

A number of organizations produce yield curves in the municipal market today, and we will look at two of them: Bloomberg and Delphis Hanover.

For most of the 20th century, municipal bond issuers had no such help beyond *The Bond Buyer* indexes to rely on as a benchmark. These remain a standard in the market, and you should be aware of them, even if you do not use them. The weekly index, created in 1917, measured the then prevailing yields on 20 municipal credits maturing in 20 years; the modern *Bond Buyer* indexes include the GO-index (where the 20 bonds are rated around a double-A), a higher-grade 11-bond index (double-A plus), a revenue bond index (the average rating is A-plus), and a one-year note index.

The problem with a single average index number is that it provides a single snapshot of what one relatively high-grade bond yields in 20 years, or a revenue bond in 30 years. What happens if you want to sell bonds maturing from 1 to 10 years, or from 1 to 15 years? Just being able to "beat" a single number is meaningless in your quest for the lowest cost financing.

A number of other indexes, like *The Bond Buyer*'s, exist—Lehman Brothers and Piper, Jaffray & Co. both put out their own indexes—but like *The Bond Buyer*'s, they are aimed primarily at apprising investors of approximate yields and are not very useful for you as an issuer.

What is useful to you is a yield curve that will enable you to gauge yields in the market across the rating and

BLOOMBERG YIELD CURVES

State Specific—South Carolina

Index		Ticker	
SOUTH CAROLINA			
1)	1 year	SCGO01	\<Indx\>
2)	2 year	SCGO02	\<Indx\>
3)	3 year	SCGO03	\<Indx\>
4)	4 year	SCGO04	\<Indx\>
5)	5 year	SCGO05	\<Indx\>
6)	7 year	SCGO07	\<Indx\>
7)	9 year	SCGO09	\<Indx\>
8)	10 year	SCGO10	\<Indx\>
9)	12 year	SCGO12	\<Indx\>
10)	14 year	SCGO14	\<Indx\>
11)	15 year	SCGO15	\<Indx\>
12)	17 year	SCGO17	\<Indx\>
13)	19 year	SCGO19	\<Indx\>
14)	20 year	SCGO20	\<Indx\>
15)	25 year	SCGO25	\<Indx\>
16)	30 year	SCGO30	\<Indx\>

maturity spectrum. The Bloomberg Fair Value Curves, for example, provide you with a daily look at yields on general obligation bonds ranging from Baa to natural and insured triple-A in grade, and from 1 to 30 years; and generic and industry-specific revenue bonds, including the education, hospital, power, utility, transportation, and general purpose sectors.

Bloomberg also carries fair value curves for taxable bonds, bank-qualified bonds, bonds subject to the alternative minimum tax, and certificates of participation. And Bloomberg carries state-specific yield curves, so if you are an issuer in South Carolina, for example, and you want to see what kinds of yields the state might

Current Value	Date	Previous Value	Date	Percent Change
3.66	6/27	3.67	6/26	-0.27
3.96	6/27	3.97	6/26	-0.25
4.16	6/27	4.17	6/26	-0.24
4.31	6/27	4.32	6/26	-0.23
4.41	6/27	4.42	6/26	-0.23
4.57	6/27	4.58	6/26	-0.22
4.73	6/27	4.74	6/26	-0.21
4.81	6/27	4.82	6/26	-0.21
4.96	6/27	4.97	6/26	-0.20
5.10	6/27	5.11	6/26	-0.20
5.16	6/27	5.17	6/26	-0.19
5.24	6/27	5.25	6/26	-0.19
5.29	6/27	5.30	6/26	-0.19
5.31	6/27	5.32	6/26	-0.19
5.35	6/27	5.36	6/26	-0.19
5.37	6/27	5.38	6/26	-0.19

command in the market, you could look up the South Carolina yield curve and find that it runs, on the day we checked it, from 3.66 percent in 1 year out to 5.37 percent in 30 years. On the same day, Louisiana, which is not rated as high as South Carolina, had yields ranging from 4.14 percent in 1 year out to 5.66 percent in 30 years *(see charts below and on pages 76–77)*.

This will give you a rough idea of what it costs the state to borrow, but you can get so much closer to what it may actually cost your municipality simply by going to the appropriate, generic category and punching up the yield curve for that category. Bloomberg terminals are relatively expensive, and chances are that you do

BLOOMBERG YIELD CURVES

State Specific—Louisiana

Index		Ticker	
LOUISIANA			
1)	1 year	LAGO01	\<Indx\>
2)	2 year	LAGO02	\<Indx\>
3)	3 year	LAGO03	\<Indx\>
4)	4 year	LAGO04	\<Indx\>
5)	5 year	LAGO05	\<Indx\>
6)	7 year	LAGO07	\<Indx\>
7)	9 year	LAGO09	\<Indx\>
8)	10 year	LAGO10	\<Indx\>
9)	12 year	LAGO12	\<Indx\>
10)	14 year	LAGO14	\<Indx\>
11)	15 year	LAGO15	\<Indx\>
12)	17 year	LAGO17	\<Indx\>
13)	19 year	LAGO19	\<Indx\>
14)	20 year	LAGO20	\<Indx\>
15)	25 year	LAGO25	\<Indx\>
16)	30 year	LAGO30	\<Indx\>

not have one, but you should be able to gain access to the Bloomberg analytics from your FA or even from your state treasurer's office.

Now we come to the Delphis Hanover Range of Yield Curve Scales, a matrix that has been put out daily since 1963. Delphis shows eight different yield curves differentiated only by rating, from natural triple-A down to Baa-minus, and going from 1 to 30 years, with 35-year and 40-year maturity also given. The levels shown represent the bid side of the market *(see chart on pages 80–81)*.

The Delphis curve also presents an "index" across the top, with triple-A at 100, and Baa-minus at 86. We

Current Value	Date	Previous Value	Date	Percent Change
4.14	6/27	4.15	6/26	-0.24
4.44	6/27	4.45	6/26	-0.22
4.59	6/27	4.60	6/26	-0.22
4.69	6/27	4.70	6/26	-0.21
4.79	6/27	4.80	6/26	-0.21
4.99	6/27	5.00	6/26	-0.20
5.09	6/27	5.10	6/26	-0.20
5.14	6/27	5.15	6/26	-0.19
5.34	6/27	5.35	6/26	-0.19
5.46	6/27	5.47	6/26	-0.18
5.50	6/27	5.51	6/26	-0.18
5.56	6/27	5.57	6/26	-0.18
5.60	6/27	5.61	6/26	-0.18
5.62	6/27	5.63	6/26	-0.18
5.64	6/27	5.65	6/26	-0.18
5.66	6/27	5.67	6/26	-0.18

Range of Yield Curve Scales
Delphis Hanover Corporation

Index	100 Aaa	98	96 Aa
1998	3.70	3.75	3.85
1999	4.00	4.05	4.15
2000	4.15	4.20	4.30
2001	4.25	4.30	4.40
2002	4.35	4.40	4.50
2003	4.45	4.50	4.60
2004	4.55	4.60	4.70
2005	4.65	4.70	4.80
2006	4.70	4.75	4.85
2007	4.75	4.80	4.90
2008	4.85	4.90	5.00
2009	4.95	5.00	5.10
2010	5.05	5.10	5.20
2011	5.10	5.15	5.25
2012	5.15	5.20	5.30
2013	5.20	5.25	5.35
2014	5.25	5.30	5.40
2015	5.30	5.35	5.45
2016	5.35	5.40	5.50
2017	5.35	5.40	5.50
2018	5.40	5.45	5.55
2019	5.40	5.45	5.55
2020	5.40	5.45	5.55
2021	5.40	5.45	5.55
2022	5.40	5.45	5.55
2027	5.45	5.50	5.60
2032	5.50	5.55	5.65
2037	5.50	5.55	5.65

Close: 06/27/97

94	92 A	90	88 Baa	86
3.95	4.05	4.20	4.35	4.55
4.25	4.35	4.50	4.65	4.85
4.40	4.55	4.70	4.85	5.05
4.50	4.65	4.80	4.95	5.15
4.60	4.75	4.90	5.05	5.25
4.70	4.85	5.00	5.15	5.35
4.80	4.95	5.10	5.25	5.45
4.90	5.00	5.15	5.30	5.50
4.95	5.05	5.20	5.35	5.55
5.00	5.10	5.25	5.40	5.60
5.10	5.20	5.35	5.50	5.70
5.20	5.30	5.45	5.60	5.80
5.30	5.40	5.55	5.70	5.90
5.35	5.50	5.65	5.80	6.00
5.40	5.55	5.70	5.85	6.05
5.45	5.60	5.75	5.90	6.10
5.50	5.65	5.80	5.95	6.15
5.55	5.70	5.85	6.00	6.15
5.60	5.75	5.90	6.05	6.20
5.60	5.75	5.90	6.05	6.20
5.65	5.80	5.95	6.10	6.25
5.65	5.80	5.95	6.10	6.25
5.65	5.80	5.95	6.10	6.25
5.65	5.80	5.95	6.10	6.25
5.65	5.80	5.95	6.10	6.25
5.70	5.85	6.00	6.15	6.30
5.75	5.90	6.05	6.20	6.35
5.75	5.90	6.05	6.20	6.35

shall see how this can be used to compare sales in Chapter 5. In addition to producing the yield curve scales, Delphis provides an in-depth pricing analysis support to issuers and FAs during their bond sales.

Yield curves are based either on yields of bonds actually trading in the market or on estimates of where the market is, so don't be confused if the yield curves you look at do not agree exactly. They are meant to give the user a good idea of where investors want yields on securities according to certain ratings and maturities. On the same day the Bloomberg Fair Value Curve listed South Carolina yields ranging from 3.66 percent to 5.37 percent, for example, Delphis listed natural triple-A rated bonds as yielding from 3.70 percent out to 5.45 percent.

The Difference between Yield and Spread

OVER THE PAST 20 years, underwriters have slashed **underwriting spreads**, or the fee you pay them to underwrite your bonds, in their competition for business. They also, unfortunately, succeeded in focusing issuers' entire attention on spread, as though nothing else mattered.

Since 1980, gross spreads on bond underwriting have declined from an average of $25 per $1,000 bond to about $7 per bond, according to Securities Data Co., which tracks such things as spreads and underwriter rankings and bond sales. Every year *The Bond Buyer* and various wire services carried stories of declining underwriting spreads, which invariably featured quotes from bankers bemoaning the matter, and more often than not blaming issuers for the state of affairs, for somehow "demanding" lower spreads.

This might not exactly have been the industry's Big Lie, but there was a certain amount of dissembling going on, because spread is not the only way in which underwriters are compensated. The fact is, as underwriters discovered in the 1980s, a whole lot more money can be made on other parts of the transaction, including, particularly, the reinvestment of proceeds. So they cut spreads even more, in some cases even waiving spreads (or, in the case of FAs, their fees) altogether if they could only get to work on the reinvestment of bond proceeds. How this gave rise to the phenomenon known as yield-burning is covered in Chapter 6. How to avoid yield-burning is addressed in Chapter 12.

The underwriters' spread happens to be one of the least important components of a deal. What really matters is good pricing and good distribution; and many underwriters, now that the yield-burning game is being shut down, are spending a lot of time trying to re-educate issuers to this fact.

Not all underwriters, however. Some underwriters are still winning business by charging spreads of $2.35 per $1,000 bond, and even lower, then following up with sloppy or inconsistent pricing, or, more precisely, pricing that appeals to buyers at your expense.

What is the buyer interested in? Yield. It is easier, after all, to sell bonds with higher yields. Why can't the $2.35 guys sell bonds at the same yields the other guys do? In some cases they can, but sometimes they can't because they simply don't have the same distribution capabilities. They win the business, and then they hog the business, and it's at your expense.

From an underwriter's point of view, this is a crazy way to operate. But it's also a particularly crazy way for you to do business.

Doing the right thing is not entirely without its risks, either. Say, for example, that you do happen to want to buck the trend and actually pay your underwriter. In exchange you also want to try to negotiate good pricing. The $2.35 guys just might go to your city council members, or county commissioners, or to the mayor, and say, How come we didn't get the business? There have even been cases where they have gone to the press and complained about such things. It is a whole lot more difficult for you to explain the art of pricing a bond and why yield is the thing to a group of politicians, or even to the press, than it is for a banker to point to the underwriter's spread and say they could have done it cheaper.

The underwriting spread is highly visible, but it is a relatively tiny portion of the "cost" of a deal. Far more important, overwhelmingly important to the terms of the deal, is the yield an issuer has to pay over the life of a bond. Just remember that 5 basis points of interest cost tacked on to a bond with a 20-year average life translates to $600,000. A bad or indifferent underwriting job can cost you millions of dollars.

◆ The Texas Public Finance Authority (TPFA) made news in 1996, when it awarded business to an underwriter for the record-low spread of $2.50 per $1,000 bond. The other underwriters who were members of the syndicate made some news of their own when they decided that the $2.50 per bond spread was unacceptable and decided to drop out.

So how did the authority fare? The $312.9 million bond deal, "did not do as well in the market as we had been expecting from a TPFA general obligation," said Sonja Suessenbach, an analyst with the Texas Bond Review Board. Suessenbach observed that the issue "was priced at or through a double-A," on the Delphis Hanover Range of Yield Curve Scales. On its previous four deals, the issuer received "nice, strong pricings through a AA1." The underwriters' spreads on those deals ranged from $3.62 to $4.51 per bond.

Bankers in Texas and elsewhere said the lesson to be learned was simple, namely that spread was a one-time cost, while yield was forever—or at least for the maturity of the bonds—and it was a mistake for issuers to concentrate on one without keeping an eye on the other.

What was the difference between yield and spread in the Texas sale? The $2.50 spread produced a total underwriter's fee of $782,250. If the authority had agreed to a $3.40 spread, which also would have been a record low but probably would have satisfied Wall Street, the underwriter's fee would have totaled $1,063,860. By cutting the spread to $2.50, the issuer "saved" $281,610. And what did the issuer's somewhat poorer showing in the market cost in terms of yield? Suessenbach estimated that it would cost the authority more than $500,000 over the life of the bonds.

Yield analytics are a very good start in learning about pricing your bond issue, but if you think your municipality is going to come to market with a negotiated deal more than once every few years, you probably will want more advanced training. The GFOA sponsors various seminars during the year, and the National Association of State Treasurers holds an annual "National Institute for Public Finance." You may even want to attend one of the more intensive training programs offered by the Municipal Issuer Research and Analysis Center (MIRAC), a nonprofit, independent research center at the University of Illinois at Chicago, which deals exclusively with municipal debt management.

MIRAC was set up in 1996 by J. B. Kurish, formerly a banker and a research director at the GFOA's Government Finance Research Center. Kurish observed upon MIRAC's launch, "Many municipal officials view the pricing of bonds as uncharted territory. The center plans to demystify the bond-pricing process by showing issuers how to gain access to relevant information and use it to their benefit." Kurish started the center with the help of a 15-member planning board, which included some of the most sophisticated issuers in the country, including James Joseph, Oklahoma's bond adviser; Frank Hoadley, Wisconsin's capital finance director; and Susan Dewey, Virginia's treasurer.

Hoadley told *The Bond Buyer*: "The ability of average issuers to understand the procedures of bond pricings and how to negotiate a sale of an issue is not very strong. Sheer talent and sheer data do not make up for the lack of a comprehensive training approach."

MIRAC does not replace the traditional FA, although it has served in that capacity. Instead, "we plan to assist issuers in evaluating their general debt status and analyzing their debt pricing," says Kurish. The center offers training programs and consulting services as well as more intensive sessions held in the weeks just before a specific bond pricing. There is an art to pricing a bond issue, and it can be taught, which is what MIRAC is all about.

Large, well-known issuers typically need little help when they come to market. They have experienced staffs and get the lowest interest rates possible simply by selling their bonds through sealed bid. Other issuers—those less well known, those with a story to tell, those with a large or unwieldy issue to sell—may find it in their interest to go the negotiated route and hire an underwriting team to sell their bonds.

Choosing Your Underwriter

IF YOU DO decide to go the negotiated route and hire an underwriting team to market and sell your bonds, you follow the same sort of RFP process described in Chapter 2 for the selection of an FA. The steps are about the same, as are the questions posed in the RFP. But pay special attention to the GFOA's "recommended practice" (also included in Chapter 2) for issuers preparing RFPs for FAs and underwriters, which was updated to include questions that the market is much more aware of right now, such as fee-splitting, other conflicts of interest, and yield-burning.

In the RFP, you are asking the underwriter to state his or her firm's experience in the municipal market and the underwriter's qualifications to sell your bond issue. You are asking the underwriting firm for ideas on innovative financing techniques, and for its selling strategy, and where it would place your bonds. You are also asking about the firm's history with the regulators. And you are laying out a few details of your own, including the terms of the engagement and the fees to be paid.

As mentioned in Chapter 2, the operative idea is to identify the best-qualified firm to sell the bonds, not to test the firm's ability to respond to an endless RFP.

An excellent place for you to learn more about this whole practice is in your own files, if your municipality has sold bonds before. Check out the responses, winning and otherwise, to the last round of RFPs your municipality sent out. They can be a real education.

If your municipality has never sold bonds before, contact your state treasurer's office, or even a nearby municipality. Chances are, they will be more than willing to show you their past RFPs and discuss how the process worked.

Selecting an underwriting team to sell your bonds does not absolve you of your responsibilities as an issuer. Ultimately, it is your job to explain your municipality's fiscal condition to investors, to lobby for a better credit rating, and to ensure that investors receive adequate disclosure about your municipality. Similarly, hiring an underwriter to sell your bonds does not free you from overseeing the entire process, and in some detail. Always remember that, ultimately, you are responsible for your municipality's bond issue.

The SEC's Paul Maco summed up the situation a few years ago: "You can't just say, 'Bring in the accountants, and the bankers, and the lawyers, and I'll go to the beach. They'll take care of everything.' I'm not aware of any case law that supports that notion." Issuers, he said, "should be careful when they hire advisers to assist them—underscore the word 'assist.'"

Chapter 5 examines the role of the underwriter, what the underwriter can and cannot do for you, and what you can do for yourself.

THE ROLE OF THE UNDER- WRITER

THE UNDERWRITER IN a negotiated bond sale is there to help you decide how to structure a bond sale and then to sell it.

The whole process of selling bonds can be likened, in a way, to space travel. With a competitive sale, you are in the position of an astronaut in one of the early Gemini capsules—essentially being shot into space on top of a rocket. There is little for you to do after the initial planning. If the market works the way it should, your sale goes off, you collect the bids, and you have your money.

With a negotiated sale, on the other hand, you're piloting the space shuttle.

A competitive sale is relatively foolproof. If buyers want your bonds, underwriters will give you a good bid for them, because they know they will be able to resell them quickly to those eager and receptive buyers. It's as simple as that.

If you really know what you are doing, however, you can negotiate at least as good a deal as you would get at competitive sale, and maybe even better. The key to a successful negotiated sale is—you guessed it—negotiation. You have to push for the best pricing possible, and, perhaps the most difficult thing of all, you have to be willing to walk away.

Pricing Municipal Bonds

AUSTIN TOBIN OF Delphis Hanover describes the interests of the parties in a course he regularly teaches on bond pricing and negotiation: "The issuer seeks the lowest possible interest rate and optimum distribution for its bonds and fair allocation among members of the underwriting syndicate. The managing underwriter seeks to eliminate risk, protect syndicate profit, and serve syndicate members and purchaser clients."

The issuer, says Tobin, "is charged with a public trust. The proper discharge of that trust obligates the issuer to demand and achieve the best price possible in the sale of its bonds. The interest of the issuer is that of the seller; the interest of the underwriter is that of the buyer."

In order to push for the best pricing possible, you have to know something about the market and how it works. The deeper you immerse yourself in the market and its ways, the better you will do with your negotiation. Tobin suggests that you become familiar with the pricing history of your previous bond sales, the changes in the bond market since your last sale, and comparable bond issue pricings, at the very least.

Before your sale, look at interest rate risk in the context of current market conditions. For at least two weeks and preferably a full month before you're ready to price your bonds, take a look at the municipal yield curve scales at the end of every day, and watch how they move. Are yields on lower grade bonds crowding yields on the high-grades? Are prices at 52-week highs? Is the ratio between 30-year tax-exempt and taxable yields below 80 percent? These three factors in combination are a sure formula for a price adjustment downward, which means that municipal yields will head higher, which in turn means that you are going to pay more to borrow money.

Familiarize yourself with the economic indicators that are scheduled to be released, and which ones traders seem to think most important. Whatever else the market follows, you follow. A decade ago the market practically came to a halt just before the Federal Reserve announced money supply figures each week. Then Commodity Research Bureau figures seemed to take center stage. Perhaps now the Consumer Price Index is the thing everyone is following. Find out what's all the rage, and watch it. Naturally, you also have to watch the mother of all markets, that for U.S. Treasury securities, which leads the way for all other fixed-income markets. When is the next Treasury bill and bond auction? In what direction have Treasury yields been moving?

Finally, look at the municipal market. What deals are on the competitive and negotiated calendars, both nationally and in your state? In other words, how crowded is the calendar? As far as institutional demand, what are they biting at? Discount paper? Zero-coupon bonds? Consider dealer inventory, as represented in Standard & Poor's daily publication, *The Blue List.* It generally runs between $1 billion and $2 billion. If it is much more than $2 billion, dealers are saturated with supply, and it is going to be that much tougher to interest them in your issue.

It takes more than attitude to negotiate a bond sale. Information is the key. If you approach it in confrontational or adversarial terms, if you somehow think you are going to "beat the rug merchant," you will lose. A lot of people in positions of responsibility find it difficult to accept that they're not experts in all fields. But you're no expert in selling municipal bonds, and no amount of bluff or bluster is going to take the place of the hard work needed to get to know the market. You have to become well versed in the nuts and bolts of market conditions, and on a daily basis, and this is going to take time. As Tobin observes, "The systematic flow of relevant information prior to and during negotiation is the key element in bond pricing, and essential to the issuer."

This may sound overwhelming. But your FA should be able to get all the information you need on a page or two and fax it to you daily.

Most FAs and public finance bankers are not very conversant in pricing; their strong suits are structuring and marketing your issue. But about a week before the actual pricing date, call your banker and ask for an indication of where the underwriter is thinking of pricing your bonds. A smart issuer will also send along his or her own preliminary ideas, in essence telling the underwriter, "This is what we want. How close can you get to it?"

Where there is cooperation between the bankers and the traders or those on the competitive underwriting desk, you will get a realistic pricing, and relatively quickly. If there is a lot of rivalry or even outright hostility between these camps, your preliminary scale will be much longer in arriving. Firms that feature cooperation rather than competition will do the best job for you.

The chart on pages 96–97 presents the progress of

a negotiation from the preliminary stages to the award. Note particularly the pricing changes in the earlier maturities. Note them, but do not be beguiled by them. Cutting a yield by 5 basis points on a one-year maturity saves you all of 33 cents per $1,000 bond, and $2.07 on a five-year maturity. For real savings, look at the longer maturities. On those longer maturities, in 15 to 20 years, you are talking about savings of $5 per bond and higher—the kind of savings that can really add up when you are selling millions of dollars in bonds.

What We Mean When We Talk About Structure

THIS IS WHERE the FAs and public finance bankers earn their money. The issuer's job, once the decision to sell debt has been made, is to get the best possible terms for the money to be borrowed, which translates into the lowest yield. The bankers and FAs help the issuer get those terms.

As noted already, the municipal bond market is highly specific; hence, there is no cookie-cutter format available for issuers to use when it comes time to sell their bonds. Even the simplest, straight vanilla bond issues require rigorous review, because bond issues must comply with a host of tax and statutory laws, not only nationally, but on a state level and even sometimes on a local level. There are rules concerning size and rules concerning debt service, and depending upon where you are, sometimes even caps on interest rates and prohibitions on the sale of bonds at a premium to par.

Issuers today, according to Paul Williams, head of municipal research at John Nuveen & Co., are torn between a "good service responsibility" and a little naiveté about what might be termed the "theory du jour." He explained, "A theory du jour is, for example,

HANDBOOK FOR MUNI-BOND ISSUERS

Progression of Negotiation

Delphis Hanover Workable Indication

UNINSURED BONDS

Maturity	05/07/93 I	05/10/93 II	05/12/93 Award
1994	2.85	2.85	2.90
1995	3.50	3.50	3.35
1996	4.00	4.00	3.90
1997	4.25	4.25	4.20
1998	4.45	4.45	4.45
1999	4.65	4.65	4.70
2000	4.85	4.85	4.85
2001	5.00	5.00	5.05
2002	5.15	5.15	5.15
2003	5.25	5.25	5.20
2004	5.35	5.35	5.30
2005	5.45	5.45	5.40
2006	5.50	5.50	5.50
2007	5.55	5.55	5.55
2008	5.60	5.60	5.60
2009			
2010			
2011			
2012	5.70	5.70	5.714
2013			
2014			
2015			
2016			
2017			
2018			

MARKUP
MARKDOWN

Underwriter Positions

UNINSURED BONDS

Maturity	Verbal 05/11/93 UWS	Scale #4 05/11/93 UWS	Scale #3 05/11/93 UWS	Scale #2 05/10/93 UWS	Scale #1 05/10/93 UWS
1994	2.90	2.90	2.90	2.90	2.90
1995	3.35	3.35	3.40	3.40	3.50
1996	3.90	3.90	3.95	3.95	4.00
1997	4.20	4.20	4.25	4.25	4.25
1998	4.45	4.45	4.50	4.50	4.50
1999	4.70	4.70	4.70	4.70	4.70
2000	4.85	4.85	4.90	4.90	4.90
2001	5.05	5.05	5.05	5.05	5.05
2002	5.15	5.15	5.15	5.15	5.15
2003	5.20	5.25	5.25	5.25	5.25
2004	5.30	5.35	5.35	5.35	5.35
2005	5.40	5.40	5.45	5.45	5.45
2006	5.50	5.50	5.50	5.55	5.55
2007	5.55	5.55	5.55	5.60	5.60
2008	5.60	5.60	5.60	5.65	5.65
2009					
2010					
2011					
2012	5.714	5.725	5.75	5.75	5.78
2013					
2014					
2015					
2016					
2017					
2018					

advance refund rather than wait for the first call, because present value savings justify it." He adds, "But, you've got to have real savings, not just a transaction for the sake of a transaction.

"It's difficult to have a long-term financial plan, because the market environment changes, and new opportunities present themselves."

New Opportunities: Swaps

NEW OPPORTUNITIES RECENTLY have included such things as interest rate swaps, where an issuer sells fixed-rate debt and then buys a derivative product called a swap, thus creating a **synthetic floating rate** for itself.

Now, what does this mean? In the simplest **interest rate swaps**, the issuer and a counterparty, usually a brokerage house or a bank, agree to exchange payment streams according to a "notional" principal amount. The principal amount is never exchanged but merely used to calculate the payment streams.

Let us say, then, that an issuer decides to take out a contract for a $100 million swap. The counterparty, let us say a bank, agrees to pay the issuer a fixed rate of 4.75 percent, and the issuer agrees to pay the counterparty an amount based on an index, say the Bond Market Association's swap index, that changes periodically. They agree that the swap will be for 10 years. They begin on an even basis, each paying the other 4.75 percent. But say the index declines, to 4.50 percent.

The issuer still must make regular, fixed, debt service payments to bondholders, of course, but if the swap is "in the money"—that is, if the amount the issuer has to pay the counterparty (4.50 percent) is less than what the counterparty has to pay to the issuer (4.75 percent)—then the issuer is able to apply that extra amount received from the counterparty to pay debt service, thus lowering the issuer's debt service payments. The issuer is paying a synthetic floating rate.

Of course, this works both ways, because rates rise and fall. What the issuer is doing in this case is speculating in the direction of interest rates as represented by the swap index. The index rises and falls, so the issuer can just as easily "lose," and finish "out of the money," and have to pay the counterparty more than he or she receives. The synthetic floating rate the issuer is paying on his or her debt can rise as well as fall, just as it can with a bond that is sold with a variable rate to begin with. Variable-rated debt is discussed in the next section.

The important thing to remember is that there is no such thing as a speculation without risk, unless you are prepared to hedge your bets (which is what the counterparty does). Bankers have an array of features you can attach to your swap, including a cap to limit just how much you will pay if your index keeps climbing. It is also crucial to remember, however, that there are fees attached to every transaction, and that every time you decide to "undo" something like a swap, it is going to cost you money.

A swap is a contract, a side bet if you will, that occurs after you sell your bonds.

Structuring your bond issue means putting together a debt service schedule and the number of serial bonds (maturing each year consecutively from the time they are sold) and term maturities (which come due 20 years or more away) it will comprise, as well as any call and redemption options.

You also have to decide whether or not you want to include things such as capital appreciation or zero-coupon bonds, which are sold to investors at deep discounts, pay no interest, but mature at a price of 100.

Or perhaps you want to sell variable-rate bonds, whose rate is reset daily, weekly, or monthly, allowing you to borrow for a long term and pay short-term rates.

Finally, there is the entire question of credit

enhancement. Bank letters of credit, bond insurance, state guarantee programs—are they available to you? How much do they cost? Remember that you must find out what any of these things means to the price of the bonds.

Sizing refers to the actual amount of the issue—how much a municipality intends to borrow. This may sound simple, but depending on the purpose of the bond issue and the locality involved, there may be limits. For example, existing bond indentures may limit or preclude entirely more debt backed by the same revenue source. There are also IRS prohibitions on overissuance. Finally, you will want to see how the new borrowing will fit into the big picture of their total outstanding debt, and into their debt management plans.

How much is too much? Standard & Poor's says, "In general, a debt burden is viewed as high when debt service payments comprise 15 percent to 20 percent of the combined operating and debt service fund expenditures."

Fixed Rate or Variable Rate?

ALL THIS BEING SAID, just as issuers generally sell bonds either of two ways, negotiated or competitive, they also sell their actual bonds in one of two formats: fixed rate or variable (floating) rate.

Variable-rate debt may have an ultimate maturity of more than 30 years, but it has a feature that allows the interest rate you pay to be adjusted on a daily, weekly, or monthly basis. The owner of the bonds also has the right, before each adjustment date, to put the security back to you in return for the owner's principal.

This is where a bank letter of credit, also known as a liquidity facility, comes in. Should bondholders inundate the issuer with their securities, the issuer uses the line of credit to pay them off.

The issuer thus gets to sell long-term debt at short-term rates. The difference can be substantial—150 basis points or more typically separates 1-year paper from 30-year paper. That's 1½ points—and millions of dollars in debt service costs.

The buyer, in return, gets a very liquid security with a flexible yield. This structure first became popular in 1984 and 1985, when tax-exempt rates were in double digits, and declined in popularity as rates declined and issuers sought to lock in fixed rates for their long-term borrowings.

Not everyone is convinced that issuers should "lock in" fixed rates. James H. White, III, the president and chief executive officer of Porter, White & Co., in Birmingham, Alabama, believes that variable-rate debt happens to be the most effective tool for issuers.

"Take a look at the tax-exempt yield curve. It is more efficient to borrow at the short end than at the long end," he says. At the short end, he points out, yields are typically 60 percent to 70 percent of taxable yields; the ratio increases to 84 percent or more on the longer maturities. He advises all of his clients to use variable-rate debt when they can, and he notes, "There is no time since 1981 when it would have been a good idea to issue fixed-rate debt versus variable-rate debt if one could do so."

White says he has been nudging his clients into shorter-duration liabilities in recent years because he has noticed that most of them have a lot of short-duration financial assets. In other words, most municipalities invest in Treasury securities maturing in a year or less.

"At the moment," White says, "we are trying to persuade the rating agencies, as well as our clients, that greater exposure to short duration liabilities is appropriate and in their interest, and actually is a risk-reducing strategy rather than a risk-increasing strategy." The rating agencies as a general rule of thumb want municipalities to limit their variable-rate issuance to 20 percent to 25 percent of their total outstanding debt, because they are concerned about the ability of issuers to make interest payments in high-interest-rate environments.

When using variable-rate debt in financing plans, White suggests observing these principles:

1 In the long term, variable-rate debt is likely to be less expensive than fixed-rate debt. If the issue can tolerate the risks associated with spikes in variable interest rates, then it can enjoy the benefits of the average lower rates associated with variable-rate debt.

2 To the extent that an issuer has a growing revenue base that is positively correlated with inflation, it can better tolerate the risks of variable-rate debt.

3 To the extent that an issuer has substantial interest-bearing assets with short average duration, then it is appropriate to enter into a risk-reducing hedge transaction in which the amount of variable-rate debt is determined in relation to the expected average amounts of short-duration assets. White thinks an efficient hedge is $1.25 in variable-rate debt for every $1 of assets in three-month Treasury bills.

Short and Shorter

WE HAVE SEEN long-term debt, where you borrow for 10, 20, 30, or even 40 years, and variable-rate debt, where you borrow for the long-term but pay short-term rates. You can also borrow in the short-term market altogether, with notes, which typically mature in one year or less.

You borrow money in the note market in order to meet cash flow needs, with tax anticipation notes (TANs), revenue anticipation notes (RANs), or tax and revenue anticipation notes (TRANs), or to provide interim financing before a bond offering, with bond anticipation notes (BANs).

Finally, there are **commercial paper programs**, which are short-term unsecured notes backed for liquidity purposes by a bank line of credit or letter of credit, with maturities of up to 270 days. These programs are used by larger issuers and provide some of the most flexible, inexpensive financing in the municipal market.

Good and Bad Underwriting

IN A GOOD UNDERWRITING, you borrow money at the lowest cost possible. A host of variables enter into the equation, the most important of which are maturity and rating. What is a good underwriting? Take another look at the Delphis scale. A good underwriting is defined by your coupons almost exactly matching, or bettering, those listed for your rating category.

This is self-evident, and it would be referred to as a "very tight" job of underwriting. What is a "bad" underwriting? The better term is probably "sloppy."

In a sloppy underwriting, had the issuer, or someone on the issuer's team, pushed a little harder, they might have gotten better terms and consequently lower costs. It is naturally easier, however, to sell higher yielding debt; and although the underwriter will try to get the best possible rates for an issuer, if the issuer doesn't seem to care, the underwriter will price the bond issue "to sell." Sometimes, the issuer, in what can only be explained as a euphoric post-sale state, will brag about it by saying that the bond issue was **oversubscribed**, which means that buyers were lining up.

If a bond issue is oversubscribed, it usually means you paid too much to begin with. And that means that the unsuspecting issuer, and the issuer's taxpayers, will wind up paying millions of dollars more in debt service, strictly because the issuer did not do his or her homework, or hire competent professionals who at least sounded the tocsin about the impending disaster. How far apart can rates be? Say your issue is a double-A plus. If your issue is priced at single-A yields—which has happened—that can mean an extra 25 or 30 basis points. And millions of dollars in extra debt service costs.

Don't Be Snowed

BANKERS WANT TO sell you stuff. In recent years, this has meant the inclusion of a wide array of products not on the menu, including variations on the basic theme of fixed- and floating-rate debt, and things such as tender option programs, synthetic advance refundings, custodial receipts, and special derivative products.

Some of these were designed to ameliorate the effects of a high-interest-rate environment; some were designed to get around tax law prohibitions; some were designed to evade constitutional limits on bonded debt; and some were designed to appeal to large, institutional buyers.

The real question issuers have to ask themselves is: Do we really need the bells and whistles?

◆ In 1989, Tampa Electric Co. signed a $25 million Municipal Forward contract with Goldman, Sachs, designer of this proprietary product. Tax-reform legislation in the early 1980s specifically prohibited advance refundings for so-called private activity bonds, to prevent two sets of bonds from being issued for the same purpose. The idea behind the "Municipal Forward" (First Boston designed a similar product called "Refunding Escrow Deposits" or REDs) was to allow issuers to lock in current rates for the time when they legally could refund their bonds. The trouble was that by the time Tampa Electric actually sold its refunding bonds in 1991, interest rates had fallen significantly. If the issuer had simply bided its time rather than enter into the Municipal Forward contract, it could have saved anywhere from 60 to 100 basis points.

Sometimes doing nothing is the smart thing to do. Unfortunately, doing nothing is not what most bankers want to hear from you. Today's lower interest rate environment has cooled a lot of bankerly creativity—but not all of it. So when you are pitched a new idea, be sure to ask questions and find out precisely how it works.

Some bankers, especially the financial engineers who tend to create new products, speak in obfuscating jargon, presenting their ideas in blocks rather than simple sentences. Many of them also grow impatient if you don't then seem to get it. Don't be intimidated. Make your bankers back up and repeat their pitch in straight English. If you still don't understand them, ask them to repeat it again, and again, and again, until you do. Make them break down their proposal into its components, and be sure to ask them how much it will cost, what the drawbacks and benefits are, and how much they will make on the deal (especially important in light of the yield-burning and other arbitrage scams, as we shall see in Chapter 6). Nothing is ever simple about these proposals, but we're not dealing with magic here, we're dealing with numbers, and the bankers, at bottom, are there to help you.

HOW TO GET INTO TROUBLE

The New Regulatory Reality

You are responsible for your bond issues. If you take away nothing else from this book but this piece of advice, then the book has paid for itself many times over.

The new regulatory reality in the municipal bond market is not that there is regulation at all—the regulations have been on the books for years—but that there is active enforcement of the rules that exist.

Federal regulators, and here we mean the SEC and the IRS, have increased their scrutiny of the market dramatically, and the result is headline news. You can get into trouble with federal regulators primarily in two ways.

First, the IRS can determine that your bonds do not comply with tax law regulations, and thus are taxable. This means that the bondholders have to pay tax on the interest they receive on your bonds. All issuers will find it in their best interest to ensure that their bonds remain tax-exempt. You don't have to, of course—but then you'll watch the lawsuits fly.

Second, as we saw in Chapter 3, you can be found guilty of fraud by not having accurately and adequately disclosed information about your municipality's financial condition in the official statement (OS) to the bond issue.

Both occurrences can cost a lot of money, both in penalties and lawyer's billable hours. You may even go to prison.

You can also get into trouble a third way, not with the federal regulators, but with the market itself. Default on your bonds, even if you are only a conduit issuer and legally not responsible for their repayment, and you can damage your reputation. A bad reputation in this market translates into a lower credit rating, higher interest costs at best, and complete lack of market access at worst. In a business where mere basis points represent millions of dollars over the lifetime of a bond issue, there is no such thing as "no-fault" public finance.

We repeat: **You are responsible for your bond issues.** This is the message the SEC and the IRS have been sending to municipalities for almost all of the 1990s. And they mean it.

IRS Scrutiny

IN 1994, THE IRS told *The Bond Buyer* that that it was focusing on four areas: "bond issues with back-loaded debt service payments that may be arbitrage-driven; guaranteed investment contracts that may have been purchased at greater than fair market value; advance refundings in which escrowed securities may have been purchased at greater than fair market value; and small-issue industrial development bonds in which the issuers may have exceeded the $10 million capital expenditure limit."

At the time, the agency also said it was investigating more than 300 municipal bond issues. Most of the problems, it appears, in one way or another revolve around what was early on dubbed yield-burning.

Yield-burning came to light in March 1995, when ex-Smith Barney banker Michael Lissack described the problem in detail to reporter Michael Quint of *The New York Times*. In simplest terms, yield-burning is no more than what bond lawyers would call "deflected" arbitrage and a clever way for bankers to earn more compensation.

Municipalities are prohibited from earning profits, or arbitrage, on the money they raise in the tax-exempt market. If you raise money at 5 percent, you cannot then invest it at 7 percent and reap the 2-percent arbitrage profit. If you do, and in some instances it is unavoidable, you must rebate that profit to the federal government. (Since 1986, municipalities have rebated more than $1.5 billion, usually as a result of imperfect investing of bond proceeds.) Almost all of the scams that have surfaced in the municipal market in recent years have, in one way or another, been about arbitrage. Yield-burning is only the latest, but it is also one of the simplest and most direct.

Lissack described one type of transaction called an **advance refunding**, in which yield-burning appears to have occurred almost systematically when conditions were right.

In such deals, municipalities sell bonds to raise money in order to pay off older, higher cost debt at its first call. That may not be for years—the first call on bonds is usually 10 years—but if the municipality wants to take advantage of a drop in rates, it sells bonds now, in advance of the actual refunding date, and reinvests the proceeds. There were many of these deals in the late 1980s and early 1990s, because interest rates came down sharply. In 1982, A-rated issuers were paying more than 14 percent to borrow money for 30 years. The same issuers are now paying a little less than 6 percent.

The money must be reinvested in such fashion so as not to produce any arbitrage profits. Municipalities can either invest the proceeds in specially designed **state and local government series Treasury securities**—SLGS, pronounced *slugs,* for short—or in Treasury securities purchased in the open market. Where they used open-market securities, dealers assembled a package of Treasury securities. If the yields on some of these securities were too high, the dealer simply raised the price, which would lower or "burn" the yield down to the right, legally allowable limit for the municipality. Lissack said the practice contributed mightily to municipal underwriters' bottom lines.

Dealers who burned down the yields pocketed the difference between what they charged and what the issuers could earn. The sum could be significant, as much as millions of dollars. In fact, it was not unheard of for certain underwriters to make more than twice the profit on the reinvestment portion of a deal than on the actual underwriting itself, thus greatly improving on those deteriorating underwriting spreads many of them complained about *(see Chapter 3).*

How much did they make? On a $471.78 million refunding done in late 1992, the Massachusetts Water Resources Authority had their underwriter, Goldman, Sachs & Co., also handle their escrow transaction. On the pricing in the primary market, the underwriter's discount on the deal was $4.28 million, or a little over

$9 per $1,000 bond. Goldman probably made about a third of that as senior managing underwriter.

On the escrow portion of the deal, using the spot prices listed in the *Wall Street Journal* on the day the escrow was purchased, the markup appears to have been $3.5 million, with the **positive cost of carry** (the earnings on the Treasuries from pricing date to the settlement date) amounting to $888,816. The grand total? $4,395,125, almost three times what the underwriter made on the deal in the primary market. Now, no one has yet called this yield-burning, but these appear to be pretty significant markups.

Markups on some other deals, using the *Wall Street Journal*–published prices, which dealers contend are inaccurate, have ranged from almost nothing to over $4 million. The reinvestment-of-proceeds business could be very lucrative. Some financial advisers who also engaged in the reinvestment business apparently even waived their fees altogether if they could also take care of the reinvestment of bond proceeds.

Remember that the issuers themselves did not lose any money under yield-burning. They had to raise the same pot of cash whether they invested it in SLGS or open-market Treasuries. Who lost? The federal government.

In July 1996, the IRS attempted to put a stop to all of this with Revenue Procedure 96-41. In the release accompanying it, the agency repeated that municipalities were prohibited from earning arbitrage profits on their tax-exempt securities transactions. But it added that they were also prohibited from arbitrarily "assigning" it elsewhere, in this case, to the dealers who worked on the reinvestment of bond proceeds, long the most private aspect of public finance.

The IRS then asked municipalities to calculate the amount of profit, or markup, and send it in, if they wanted to avoid further enforcement action and concomitant penalties. The IRS gave municipalities one year to figure out what they owed, and the clock began running. Some observers thought the total liability might run to as much as $1 billion, although, at this writing, that seems to be on the high side.

The uproar was inevitable, and predictable. Municipalities and their representative lobbyists (the National League of Cities, the National Association of State Treasurers, and the GFOA, among others) complained vociferously to both the Treasury and the IRS that holding them responsible for yield-burning was unfair. After all, they said, they did not make any profits on their transactions. Underwriters and dealers did.

Municipal lobbyists contended that issuers did not know about yield-burning and simply relied on their underwriters, lawyers, and financial advisers, and on their written certifications and representations that the prices they paid for their investments was reasonable and legal. In other words, the municipalities trusted their professionals, and more often than not trusted them implicitly, without really pulling apart the transactions to check their accuracy.

The government, the lobbyists said, should go after the dealers. For its part, the IRS listened and put the one-year "closing agreement" deadline on indefinite hold. As this book went to press, the IRS was still huddling, with the SEC, among other parties, to determine the next step. It seems unlikely that the IRS will rescind its measure, however. In fact, various IRS officials have said they see yield-burning as a moneymaker for the agency. The IRS's mission, after all, is to collect taxes, and it is expected to seize every opportunity to do so.

Several analysts thought that the situation would be resolved by the two agencies working together, with the IRS calculating what a municipality owes, and the SEC going after the offending underwriter, financial adviser, or investment provider, for restitution. The problem with this scenario is that the two agencies have vastly different goals. The IRS collects money owed to the government and is eager to prosecute as many cases as possible. The SEC, on the other hand, usually brings one or two enforcement actions designed to define the lines of the law.

What was more than a little troubling about the whole business of yield-burning, however, was that it appeared that not all issuers were exactly unmindful of what was going on. In other words, some of them were quite complicit in the proceedings.

Why? For a variety of reasons. There were issuers who were indeed completely clueless, who never bothered to track the reinvestment of proceeds, and who relied on the representations of their professionals.

There were also issuers who resented the IRS rules prohibiting them from earning arbitrage on bond proceeds as unnecessarily time-consuming and onerous in the first place. Still others indicated that they knew they were being burned, but that it also seemed to be part of accepted industry practice, and in addition, as part of the price to be paid for lower underwriting spreads, a very visible part of most bond transactions.

Yet others were sold on what would come to be known as yield-burning by their own financial advisers as a way to compensate and provide incentive to their underwriters, "at no additional cost" to themselves.

Finally, it seemed that some municipal officials allowed it to go on, because they wanted jobs as bankers at underwriting firms when their days as public officials were over, and did not want reputations as troublemakers.

None of these are particularly good reasons in the eyes of the IRS, which in 1997, at least, seemed fairly intent on getting the money it was owed.

Dealers, for their part and as represented by their lobbying group, the Public Securities Association, countered that market volatility, among other things, made it impossible to set a benchmark price for Treasury securities. Therefore, they reasoned, each transaction would have to be examined on a case-by-case basis. This defense was called "absurd on its face," by critics, who added that dealers certainly knew what the profit on a transaction was.

It is still unclear exactly how widespread yield-burning was, and what the markups amounted to, but it is absolutely clear that it is going to cost the market, both issuers and the industry, a pretty penny. The market's participants have so far probably spent in excess of $50 million simply in responding to requests by the IRS and the SEC for information.

Although most of the stories about yield-burning have centered around advance refunding transactions, you would be greatly mistaken if you believed it ended there. In fact, yield-burning seems to have occurred on a wide variety of municipal investments. The key is to think of it less in terms of yield-burning and more as simple overcharging for a variety of municipal investments, most but not all of which take place directly after bond sales. Ways of avoiding such problems are discussed in Chapter 12.

How did it come to this? As Public Financial Management's F. John White said,

> Once you get beyond the top 50 issuers, you're dealing with people who don't issue bonds for a living. Bond issues are something they do once every few years. That's why firms like ours exist. A bond issue to them is just a hassle. They usually have some elected official telling them how to make up the management group, and who the bond counsel should be—to them it's just a big hassle.

Yet the IRS's unwelcome scrutiny proves that you have to keep your eye on the ball, not just at the bond sale, but after the bond sale, as well. Two very underrated words in the municipal market are: Pay attention.

THE

BOND
COUNSEL

THE BOND COUNSEL is a lawyer who opines upon the security, legality, and tax-exemption of the issue.

Who They Are, and Why They Exist

BOND COUNSEL ROSE to prominence at the turn of the 20th century, after municipalities that had sold bond issues sought to get out of their obligation to repay, claiming that they never had the legal authority to enter into such financings in the first place. They sought, to use the Latin, legal expression, *ultra vires* means to void their contractual agreements with bondholders, who soon found it in their best interest to buy only bonds that also had opinions from lawyers attached to them stating that the bond issue was legal.

It was not uncommon in the early years of the 20th century for such legal opinions to be attached separately to the actual bonds for which they were given, rather than bound into the preliminary and final official statements as an appendix, the way they are today.

As late as 1917, *The Bond Buyer,* as the weekly *Bond Buyer* was then known (to distinguish it from *The Daily Bond Buyer*), observed, "Municipalities, perhaps, do not appreciate the practical value of a legal opinion in the marketing of a bond. Bond dealers . . . would do well to educate the American municipality to the custom of having all bonds approved as to legality by a recognized bond attorney prior to the original offering of the issue." The newspaper even editorialized that the matter of the legal opinion "seems to us to be one of the 'loose ends' of the municipal bond business that needs attention."

It is a loose end no more, and no issuer today would think of coming to market without a legal opinion, and one provided by a recognized bond counsel, listed in *The Bond Buyer's Municipal Marketplace,* which is known as the **Red Book** because of its cover's color. Some issuers have experimented with using a state attorney general's opinion, and the Port Authority of New York and New Jersey uses its own general counsel's opinion, but most issuers will find it in their best interest to retain private bond lawyers who are familiar with public finance in their states.

Questionable Practices

IN CHAPTER 1 WE NOTED two trends that have caused havoc in the municipal market in recent years: playing politics by loading up bond issues with multiple professionals, and price-cutting. Both practices have infected the field of bond law.

In 1988, the Special Committee on Standards and Practice of the National Association of Bond Lawyers (NABL) produced a report entitled *Lawyer Proliferation in Public Finance Transactions*. The NABL committee reported: "The Committee observes that the employment of co-bond counsel today seems to be largely motivated by socioeconomic or political factors, or by the wish of various lawyers to obtain exposure, name recognition and legal fees (as well, presumably as expertise) in what is perceived—correctly or not—to be a lucrative field of the law."

The committee continued, "We must also observe that . . . co-bond counsel today often do not bring much, in the way of relevant expert or critical services, to the transaction. As noted above, the bond counsel field is a field in which it is difficult at best to become expert, without actually doing the work." And the committee concluded:

> We believe that some co-bond counsel apparently want to participate in public financing transactions primarily to collect a fee and neither expect nor wish to render any legal services other than copying and signing a legal opinion in the form that lead counsel has prepared. We believe that others are fully content to render more-or-less routine and less meaningful services and have little if any wish to achieve the expertise that will enable them to act as sole bond counsel in a public financing transaction. In some of these latter cases, these co-bond counsel may be so motivated because they frankly do not want to devote the time and energy to achieve full proficiency; and in still others, because they do not wish to expose themselves to the substantial liability of sole bond counsel.

Naming numerous co-counsel to a transaction is nothing more than playing politics; it has nothing to do with getting the lowest interest rates on your bonds. Hiring co-counsel is like hiring two or three different, competing electricians to do some work on your home. It makes no sense.

No less a problem among bond lawyers is the business of price-cutting. In early 1995, for example, New York City put out an RFP for special disclosure counsel. The RFP stated that the city wanted the "highest quality legal services," but then spelled out the first minimum qualification: "Price proposals may not exceed the following hourly rates—$150 for a partner, $100 for an associate and $30 for a paraprofessional."

One critic told Grant's *Municipal Bond Observer* that those words stopped him cold. "Where are they going to find a major New York City law firm where the partners charge only $150 an hour for complicated legal work?" he asked. "A competent divorce lawyer from Tom's River, New Jersey, charges $275 an hour. A bond lawyer who is a partner at a New York City law firm charges at least $500 an hour."

This critic continued, "Is it right for a public agency to demand a loss leader? That's some business for a law firm to remain in. Perhaps a firm will agree to work for $150 an hour for New York City because of the prestige of the client. What does the firm do—charge for three hours for every one? Make it up on the fees they charge other clients? Is that fair to the other municipal clients? And is this any way to ensure that the city and its bondholders are getting the highest quality legal services?"

A Texas bond lawyer said much the same thing, that a law firm will do one of three things when presented with such an RFP: "Either you pad the time or you do less than necessary. Or you lose your shirt." He then recounted the following tale: His firm had chosen the third option and was examining the issuer's documents. He noticed that the issuer kept one of its reserve funds in 30-day Treasury securities. When he asked why, the issuer told him that he thought that the rating agencies required it. The lawyer doubted the explanation and then asked, "Where would you put that money if you didn't have to put it in 30-day paper?" The client said he would probably invest it in higher yielding Treasury securities with a maturity of one year. The lawyer recommended that he do so, and that if the rating agency had any concerns, they would address them at the time. The move wound up saving the client several million dollars.

The issuer came back to market the following year and sent out an RFP. The lawyer's firm was not chosen, and when he asked the issuer why, he was told, "Price."

Several states are looking at removing price as the deciding consideration from the RFP process. They are looking particularly at an Arkansas law, on the books since 1989 and amended in 1995 to include all "professional services," designed to eliminate bidding contests.

The Arkansas model, in statutes 19-11-801, 802, states:

> It is the policy of the State of Arkansas and political subdivisions that the state and political subdivisions shall negotiate contracts for professional services on the basis of demonstrated competence and qualifications for the type of services required and at fair and reasonable prices and to prohibit the use of competitive bidding for the procurement of professional services. . . . If the political subdivision is unable to negotiate a satisfactory contract with the firm selected, negotiations with that firm shall be terminated. The political subdivision shall then undertake negotiations with another of the qualified firms selected.

When you go shopping for bond counsel, the most important considerations are professionalism and good ideas. The least important factor is price. You get what you pay for. And speaking of paying, we next turn our attention to those you want to pay for your bonds, the buyers.

CHAPTER

WHO BUYS YOUR BONDS?

THAT THE MUNICIPAL bond market is mainly retail is one of its many cherished myths. The truth is that the municipal bond market is almost entirely institutional by nature.

There are many reasons why this is so, but that it *is* so is undeniable. Retail investors may ultimately benefit from tax-exempt interest to the extent that they hold municipal bonds and municipal bond mutual funds. But they are not interested in the municipal market, and those who are interested make up a very small club.

Retail, however, is not interested in municipal bonds the way it is interested and engaged, almost culturally, in the stock market. For one thing, the price of admission is relatively high. Investors can participate in the stock market for as little as a few hundred dollars. To participate in the municipal bond market, and by that we mean buying bonds, not shares in mutual funds, they need $25,000 or $50,000.

Nor are municipal bonds even part of the financial popular culture. They do not trade on a central exchange. Their prices are not carried in daily newspapers. The players in the market are rarely, if ever, seen on television or written up even in the financial press. Retail investors may buy your bonds, but they are not very interested in you or your bonds, unless you stop paying them and go into default. The low default rate—approximately 2 percent—further reinforces their indifference.

Make no mistake. The household sector does hold the second largest chunk of the $1.3 trillion in municipal bonds outstanding—$416 billion, according to the Federal Reserve's quarterly, *Flow of Funds Accounts of the United States*. But funds, including mutual funds, money market funds, and closed-end funds, in fact hold the largest amount, $432 billion. Property and casualty insurance companies come in third, with more than $170 billion. Commercial banks and trust companies hold a combined $200 billion.

The Players

IT'S ALL WELL AND GOOD to talk about billions here and billions there, but the fact remains that you could probably pull all the major players of municipal bonds, that is, the major buyers, together in the barroom at Harry's at Hanover Square, a restaurant located just south of Wall Street and favored by municipal bond dealers. There are, perhaps, 200 major buyers.

How does one court this elite community? Through the time-honored "dog and pony show," of course. If your issue is big enough, and if you come to market frequently enough, you must make it your business to go on a regular tour to meet your investors, for either one-on-one meetings or group meetings.

The tour, which is usually done in advance of a bond sale, can take a week or two, and should make stops in Boston, New York, Philadelphia, Chicago, Minneapolis, and San Francisco, which is where the fund companies are concentrated. And if you have buyers in Denver, or Hartford, or Kansas City, or San Antonio, well, you should go there, too, and sit down for an informational bull session with the buyer and his research staff. And if you're really, really big—big enough to sell taxable municipal bonds abroad—you might even venture to Europe or Japan to do the same thing. Your financial adviser (FA) or investment banker will help you with your itinerary; selling bonds and selling you is what they excel at.

Of course, how far you go depends a lot on size. If you are like most issuers (i.e., small), you have a very local constituency, consisting of a local bank or two and an in-state mutual fund company. To meet with them, you just go down to the country club. If you are like most issuers, you will sell your small, usually straight-vanilla bond issue competitively, and it will be bought by a local, regional underwriter.

But say you're a larger issuer, one who intends to come to market at least once a year, and with $40 million, $50 million, or $100 million issues or larger. You become national, in what we have seen is a largely regional market. Who will buy your bonds? As we have seen, this is a market not of the bland generalization, but of the specific and of the particular when not of the outright peculiar. But one Massachusetts authority issue of several hundred million dollars

Who Buys Your Bonds?

(1st quarter holdings of municipal securities, by sector)

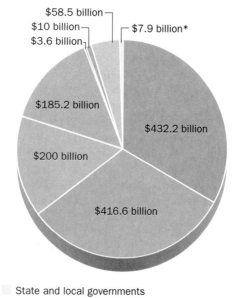

$58.5 billion
$10 billion
$3.6 billion
$7.9 billion*
$185.2 billion
$432.2 billion
$200 billion
$416.6 billion

State and local governments
Nonfinancial corporation
Brokers and dealers
Government-sponsored enterprises
Insurance companies
Banks
Households
Funds

*Charted at 12 o'clock
position; other sectors
follow counterclockwise

INSTITUTIONS, including those which manage municipal bonds held by individual investors, dominate the market.

SOURCE: FLOW OF FUNDS ACCOUNTS OF THE UNITED STATES

some years back was divided up with about 46 percent of it going to bond funds, 20 percent going directly to retail investors, and another 20 percent going to insurance companies. The remainder was carved up among bank trust departments, investment counselors, and assorted corporate buyers. Dealers bought 2 percent of it for their inventories. This is fairly typical for a fairly large bond issue.

How will your bonds be distributed nationally? Again, using the Massachusetts issue as an example, fully 40 percent of the deal went to New York, 20 percent to Illinois, 13 percent to California, and 5 percent to Pennsylvania. Approximately 20 percent of the issue remained in Massachusetts. This too seems typical for a fairly large bond issue.

No one appreciates surprises in the municipal market. What will your investors ask? First, they will want to get comfortable with the credit and its structure, if you are a first-time issuer. After that, they will want regular updates on your condition and your future plans. At some point you or your banker or FA will then ask them The Question about whether they are interested in the credit. Will they buy your bonds? What are they looking for?

And here is a sampling of what the buyers told our Massachusetts issuer:

"Look at five- to six-year range; approximately $500,000 in terms, whichever term is cheaper."

"Price-sensitive; could buy $10 million to $40 million non-callable terms."

"Questions about credit—call bond counsel to clarify."

"Could buy, but not sure about tone of market."

"Will not buy—full on Massachusetts credits and not in market for municipals."

"Will probably buy 6 percent–6.5 percent coupons."

"Will buy only if insured."

"May look at non-callable terms."

"Expected to buy $5 million long."

"May buy serials."

"Credit approved."

This fine range of answers goes a long way toward explaining why the market is the way it is. Some investors like serial bonds, others like term bonds. Some want insurance; some want yield; others want non-callable zero-coupon bonds. Good bankers and FAs can help you structure your issue to cater to their needs, within reason.

The key to success, whether you are a big or small issuer, is getting as wide a distribution as possible for your bonds. Here's what one issuer did about it.

"The Evil Syndicate"

FRANK HOADLEY, Wisconsin's director of capital finance, in 1997 described what he called "The Evil Syndicate." He observed, "Syndicates, as currently drawn up, are nothing more than a risk-minimization strategy for underwriters."

The result, he said, was that most of the state's bonds were sold to a relative handful of investors: 15 institutions own half of the state's $3.3 billion in outstanding general obligation bonds, with one investor holding 25 percent.

Hoadley's solution? Set up an incentive pot. "The purpose of the pot is to encourage syndicate members to go out and call on specific investors who have not bought the state's bonds before." More investors, of course, mean more competition for the state's bonds, and more competition usually means lower interest costs and lower borrowing costs in the years ahead.

Other Strategies

THE DREAM OF BOND ISSUERS everywhere is to expand the base of bond buyers for their debt. They have pursued this goal through a variety of means, but chief among them, naturally enough, is what might be termed the chase for the retail buyer.

This is hardly new; more than a hundred years ago, Chicago attempted to broaden its investor base by opening a municipal bond window in city hall to encourage the walk-in trade. More recently, some municipalities have experimented with "mini-bonds" in denominations of from $100 to $1,000 (although a municipal bond is in theory $1,000, they are most commonly sold in lots of $5,000, and most dealers prefer to work in amounts of $25,000 to $50,000).

Even more recently, some municipalities have insisted that a special "retail order period" precede the actual day of sale, so that all retail orders could be filled, and not crowded out by institutions. These are invariably called great successes after the sale. In fact, however, actual average retail participation in the larger issues remains about the same as it has been for the past several years: 20 percent.

Yet the idea of trying to reach retail is a good one, simply because there are so many potential retail customers out there. If you want to reach them, however, it is going to cost more. A Michigan bond lawyer recently advised a client not to blanch at a $22 per bond underwriting spread, and to pay it if she thought it resulted in (a) the issuer's bonds being to be sold to retail, and (b) some real risk-taking (i.e., actual underwriting on the part of the underwriting syndicate).

The bond lawyer observed, "Issuers have got the spread down, but in the long run they are paying as much as 20 basis points more in yield, because they're being sold to funds and unit investment trusts and the like. There's no retail market left for most municipal bonds, because they're not paying underwriters to underwrite, to take risk."

The lawyer continued, "Issuers can reduce their yields dramatically, if they agree to pay a little higher underwriter spread. The trouble is, issuers can see the spread right there in the bond documents. It becomes a political thing. It's a little tougher to visualize yield."

Now that we have discussed sales, it is time to discuss salesmanship of another kind.

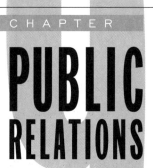

CHAPTER

PUBLIC
RELATIONS

WE HAVE CONSIDERED selling the bonds negotiated, and selling the bonds competitive; selling the bonds to institutions, and selling the bonds to retail; and how to sell bonds the right way, and how to sell bonds the wrong way. Now it is time to consider how to sell bonds at all, meaning: how to sell bonds to the voters, and how to sell bonds to the press.

How to Win Bond Elections

A FORMER NEW JERSEY bond issuer recently advised: "I always found that if there was organized opposition to a general obligation bond issue on the ballot, that it would fail."

These are days of angry voters, of initiative and referendum, of rebellion against taxes, and of resentment toward government spending. These are days of activist oldsters who organize to oppose new bond issues for schools. You must assume today that there is always going to be at least some organized opposition to a new bond issue, varying only in intensity. What to do?

This being the municipal market, the answer naturally relies more on art than on science. It was once thought, for example, that holding a special election for a bond issue favored its passage. The theory was that supporters could be more easily mustered than opponents. This is no longer the case.

Take school bonds, for example. More bonds are sold for the purpose of "education," year in and year out, than any other sector except the catchall category of "general purpose." School bonds are perhaps the purest example of general obligation bond financing. Who could possibly be against more funding for education?

A lot of people, it turns out. Those with children who are grown and those without children at all may object to paying for something they will not use. Even those demographically desirable voters with school-age children may send them to private schools, and so regard public school funding almost as a variety of double taxation. Finally, as Susan MacManus, a professor of public administration and political science at the University of South Florida, wrote in *Government Finance Review* magazine, "Analysts studying why school tax and bond proposals fail have concluded that a sizable portion of the population believes that schools are inefficient, ineffective, and unaccountable."

There is no magic bullet when it comes to winning school bond elections, or any other kind of bond elections, for that matter. But we can point out what seems to have worked.

Winning a bond election is like winning any other election. It requires extensive, expensive campaigning. Bond issues that somehow materialize on ballots with no or very limited explanation are bond issues designed to fail. To use a bit of New Age management-speak, bond issues need champions.

Nobody wants higher taxes. But people do want services, and they will pay for what they see as direct benefits. As analyst Hy Grossman of Standard & Poor's pointed out in an article in Standard & Poor's *Credit-Week Municipal,* a weekly publication of the rating agency: "Despite widespread campaigns by states and local governments to restrain or cut employee head-counts, shifting priorities in recent years have resulted, in the aggregate, in public employment outpacing the growth in the general population." He added, "The trend is uneven among the states, reflecting individual priorities among the public policy choices, including fiscal restraint and prudence, even in an expanding economy producing higher-than-anticipated revenues."

The key to getting bonds approved, then, is getting the voters to see the direct connection between the bonds and those benefits, and this has to be the heart of the campaign. Most people, believe it or not, do not think about municipal bonds, or the bond market. Municipal bonds have to be explained, carefully and in detail. And they then have to be championed—a few articles on newspapers' op-ed pages, or a few letters to the editor, simply will not do. To get the message out, you have to pay for advertising on radio and television, and convince what MacManus called "the conditional voters," those who fall into neither the supporters' nor the opponents' camps.

You also must get the word out to groups that are supportive of the bond issue in the first place, and get them energized about it. You know the opposition will be getting their troops out. In 1997, the San Ysidro, California school district passed a $250 million school bond issue, then the largest local school bond measure in the history of the state. How did it pass? "Every faction came together. They were all represented on the campaign committee," *The San Diego Union-Tribune* reported. The paper said that a consultant hired for the election "targeted 1,900 voters who regularly voted in previous elections and followed up with phone calls to likely supporters. And the campaign encouraged people to vote absentee because of the special nature of the election."

As MacManus also points out, successful bond proposals seem to enjoy grassroots support, rather than the infatuation of a community elite. Finally, she notes that persistence is a virtue. If your bond proposal does not succeed the first time out, keep trying.

To put things into perspective, however, it is important to realize that comparatively few of the bonds sold every year, at least in terms of dollar volume, are approved by the voters. The rise of independent authorities and revenue bonds, as noted in Chapter 1, has meant more municipal revenue bond issuance, and especially more non–voter-approved bond issuance.

The volume of bonds submitted to the voters in the modern age of municipals (which we will here define as over the past 15 years) has climbed to an average of roughly $15 billion annually; on average, almost 70 percent have been approved by voters. Even if voters approved 100 percent of the bonds on the ballots each year, and those bonds were also sold (highly unusual: it may take four or five years to sell the bonds approved by voters in any given year), they would make up less than 10 percent of the dollar volume of bonds sold.

The Press (Here's What You're Up Against)

THE MUNICIPAL MARKET has a problem with the press, and that is the press's fault. The municipal market, simply put, is nobody's beat.

And that is too bad. Here is a market of $1.3 trillion, that intrudes into the life of every American, that is undergoing dramatic transformation owing to regulation and prosecution, that has a Dickensian cast of characters, and it is virtually ignored by the press. Even in public finance—the various meetings where the political decisions are made to sell bonds —when it is covered at all, it is covered badly.

The enemy, frankly, is youth. Most newspapers assign their youngest reporters to city council meetings and the like, and it falls to these youngest reporters to sort out the practice and process of public finance. Their seniors—the bureau chiefs, editors, and copyeditors who assign them, guide them, and shape their stories for inclusion in the next day's paper—are no better. Chances are, they got out of covering public finance as soon as they could.

In the municipal market, experience counts, and inexperience costs. The process is involved at best. The industry is clubby, highly dependent on insiders' jargon, and more than a little suspicious of reporters who, it figures, are going to "get it wrong," anyway. It is no easy task to figure out, and then write about, what is going on in a municipal transaction, especially for those who do not have a grounding in either business or finance.

Youth is the enemy, and yet reporting is by its nature a young person's game. The craft encourages people to move on, from paper to paper. It encourages them not to specialize. And, finally, it discourages them from being reporters for too long. The money, and any perks of a lifetime in journalism, are concentrated in a very few top editing positions. The result is that by the time a reporter has a working knowledge of one beat, he or she is generally off to the next, or off to another paper entirely. Or he or she may rise through the ranks, which means editing copy rather than reporting or writing it any more.

On top of all of this, of course, municipals have been painted as boring. A reporter can stumble on a great municipal bond story, recognize it as such, report it, and even begin writing it, and still have a very tough time convincing an editor to run it—all because it's about municipal bonds. Editors want to run stories that they think will be of interest to their readers, and it is their perception that municipal finance is not one of them.

They also want to run stories that, for the most part, can be summarized in very few words—what's called the "nut graf" for short, which says, "Here's what this story is about." This can lead to oversimplification, which is why most municipal bond stories you read in the press are either very shallow and full of holes, or exercises in broad generalization.

Then there are one-source stories, or stories that state the obvious in scandalous terms, or stories that wrongheadedly discuss the municipal bond market in terms of the stock market.

There are even professionals in the municipal market who fall back on equity terms to describe the municipal market. They will say, for example, that prices on a particular bond are "hit hard" in reaction to some piece of news, which will be duly reported by the reporter on the other end of the line. In reality, municipal bond prices barely move. They seem to be bulletproof and practically invulnerable to bad news that would otherwise flatten a stock's price in a trading session. When municipal bonds do move, they rise or fall en masse, and entirely in line with the Treasury market.

What really happens to bond prices on bad news? The bid side may dry up for a while, which means that those who want to sell such securities are at least temporarily out of luck. Or it may not.

What should you watch for? Unless you are called by one of the handful of experienced municipal market journalists out there, and there are a few (probably fewer than three dozen, nationally), you essentially will be faced by two kinds of reporters: The first is an eager youngster who will write what he or she is told in uncritical fashion, without understanding or questioning. The second is what might be termed an assassin.

The first reporter is more common by far. This reporter can be gulled by a simple press release, and perhaps a call from your banker or FA, or even yourself. He or she does not so much report a story as transcribe it.

Consider the case of the phantom savings. In 1995, the town of Babylon, New York did an $80.2 million advance refunding coupled with an interest rate swap. The local newspaper, *Newsday,* carried a story headlined "Babylon OKs Debt Swap to Lower Interest Costs." *The Bond Buyer* carried a story, "In Taxable-to-Tax-Exempt Swap, Babylon, N.Y., Saves $8.5 Million."

In fact, as an analysis of the situation showed, there was no "savings." The issuer, depending on how you looked at it, took out a loan of either $8.5 million at 7.35 percent, or $20.9 million at 14.25 percent. The banker who worked on the deal admitted to me six months later, "As I remember it, the savings from the refunding would have been $8.5 million, but they did not want it over time. They wanted it up front, and paid a swap rate higher than it would have been normally" in order to get it.

It is not difficult to get this kind of story in the press, however, because editors respond to stories about "savings." As for sorting it all out, most reporters simply do not have the time or analytical tools, let alone the inclination, to do so. The key word to watch for in these kinds of stories is complex. If a reporter describes something as "complex" or "unusually complex," it usually means that he or she is not going to take the time to pull the thing apart and see what makes it tick.

Unfortunately, this could be the kind of coverage you want, depending on your scruples. If you are putting together a transaction that, for example, allows you to balance your budget by taking long-term savings as an up-front loan, you can do so and 9 times out of 10 fool the press. Sometimes there is no way to analyze a transaction without the cooperation of the bankers who put it together, and if they "decline to give further details," as many do, it will be monstrously difficult for the reporter to figure it out. Relatively few reporters will go back and use the Freedom of Information Act to write a story about a transaction that is months old.

What is the harm? This kind of "trade journalism" is bad because in essence it promotes the trade, at the expense of the truth. It is photocopied, passed around, and used as a piece of marketing by the participants in the deal to get more and similar business, under similarly false pretenses.

Not long ago, a group of bankers told the then-editors of *The Bond Buyer* they thought it would be a good idea for the newspaper to carry stories explaining the derivatives market to issuers, and how the judicious use of derivatives could save them money. On the surface this was true; however, what they really wanted was not critical reporting, but marketing. What they got, at least for a time, was critical reporting.

The second kind of reporter you're likely to meet is the assassin. This invariably angry and unpleasant journalist proceeds from the notion that, if it's the municipal market, something illegal or unethical must be taking place. With this kind of reporter you are likely to get a piece of work that is unbalanced at best and dishonest at worst. But just as editors respond to stories about "saving the taxpayers' money," they also respond to stories about scandal—"stealing the taxpayers' money," if you will. If there's nothing to get the sense of popular outrage going, as the saying goes, then there's no story.

This kind of reporter is far rarer than the first. More often than not, this reporter's mind is already made up: In other words, you are guilty until proven innocent.

The role of a free press in a democracy, said H. L. Mencken, is to "disagree with everything, disbelieve everyone, and generally raise hell." Herbert Bayard Swope, editor of the now-defunct *New York World,* once said that "the function of a good reporter is not to cover a story, but to uncover it." Joseph Pulitzer once wrote, "There is not a crime, there is not a vice which does not live in secrecy. Get these things out in the open, describe them, attack them, ridicule them in the press and sooner or later public opinion will sweep them away." These are not words journalists take lightly.

The solution? Kill them with kindness. The best policy is to insist that the reporter come in and meet with you, then describe your proposed financing simply and systematically. You have to get your side of the story out.

Having sold the press, we now proceed to the day of the sale.

WHAT HAPPENS IN A
BOND
SALE

FIXED OR FLOATING-RATE, negotiated or competitive, rated or unrated, we proceed now to the sale. Presale preparation is key in both instances.

What to Do Before a Competitive Sale

Advertising. Depending on local ordinance, you must take out an advertisement, in either a local newspaper or a national one, such as *The Wall Street Journal* or *The Bond Buyer,* announcing the terms of the transaction and its various call provisions, as well as when and where sealed bids will be taken. The issue must also be put on dealers' calendars, and listed with *The Bond Buyer* and the news wires. Bloomberg, Reuters, Dow Jones, and the Thomson Municipal News wire service, formerly known as the Munifacts newswire, all carry calendars listing competitive and negotiated bond deals.

Marketing. Copies of the preliminary official statement (OS) should be sent out to potential investors as a way to drum up interest in the new issue.

The Big Day

THE ACTUAL DAY of the sale is anticlimactic. You collect good-faith deposit checks or other electronic commitments from bidders, then open and evaluate the bids. This is a bare-bones description, but the process is relatively simple and straightforward.

On a negotiated sale, you have already participated in the blitz of presale marketing, orchestrated by your underwriter. The actual day of the sale is referred to as the day of the pricing, because most of the actual "sale" work has been done in the days and weeks prior. Underwriters have already discussed in general terms about where yields will be with institutional buyers. If you have followed the advice laid out in Chapter 4, you should also have a good idea where yields will be.

It is important to understand what goes on the day of the pricing, but this is the relatively foolproof part of the process. You do not, as a rule, get into trouble because of what happens the day of the sale. You get into trouble well before, either in agreeing to sell bonds for an unfeasible project in the first place, or in choosing teams of incompetent or untrustworthy professionals, or directly after, when the proceeds of the sale are reinvested. The day of the sale is not the time for you to feel you have to yell "Stop the music!" By the day of the sale, you understand the process. You are accustomed to the tune.

Most people, to the extent they think about bond underwriting at all, imagine it to be an involved process where bonds are priced, allotted to various syndicate members, and then sold. In reality what happens is that, in a short period of time, two hours at most, the bonds are priced, the orders are filled, the bonds are "sold," and the cake is cut. What is really divided up among the underwriters are not "the bonds," but money, in the form of profits.

Components of the Underwriter's Spread

HERE A WORD is in order about the various components of underwriter's spread, discussed in detail in Chapter 2. These are the management fee, paid to the underwriter for investment banking services; expenses; underwriting fee (or risk); and takedown.

The **takedown** is the sales commission, and with the exception of the takedown, the other segments of the spread should be agreed to beforehand. There should be no surprises at this point, although not a year goes by that some official, somewhere, asks me about whether or not a $70 per bond underwriting spread is reasonable (it is not; in fact, it is absurdly high), or if $250,000 in "computer expenses" is justified (it is difficult to believe so).

In the past, underwriters and other parties to the transaction have been able to bury a wide variety of fee income in such fashion. But those days are coming to an end as issuers and their representatives become more astute in the ways of the market, and also remember to ask more questions about where the taxpayers' money is going.

ONE OF THE HOTTEST issues in public finance during the mid-1990s was "Who owns the takedown?" The underwriters believed they did, because they always controlled the takedown—in other words, they dictated where the profits went. The buyers, on the other hand, came to believe that they owned the takedown and could designate how the sales credit was divided up, rewarding firms that provided them with the best service, which often included making a market when they, the buyers, needed one. But by the mid-1990s, issuers got to thinking it was their right to direct who got the money, and so the more politically attuned began stipulating that the bookrunning manager put aside a certain percentage of the profits to be distributed to, for example, minority- or women-owned firms.

It was an interesting question, and continues to be. The GFOA, in its 1994 booklet *Pricing Bonds in a Negotiated Sale: How to Manage the Process,* observes: "There often is a trade-off between policy goals and costs. Generally, special distribution requirements run counter to efficient distribution, adding to the issuer's cost of borrowing."

There are goals, and there are goals, and some are commendable. Wider distribution of an issuer's bonds is one; so is distribution to retail with a special retail-order period; so are sales to in-state clients first. They all may cost a little extra up front but well worth the issuer's while and pay benefits in the long run.

How are bond orders placed? There are group net orders, net designated orders, and member orders. With **group net orders**, the sales commission is paid to all members of the syndicate. **Net designated orders** allow buyers to specify which underwriters will be paid sales commissions, but usually stipulate that at least three firms must be designated, that no firm may receive more than 50 percent of any designation, and that no firm may receive less than 10 percent of any designation. Issuers sometimes direct that at least one minority- or woman-owned firm be designated on such orders, or that a certain percentage of the takedown be deposited into a pool to be allocated according to the issuer's discretion. Finally, there are **member orders**, which firms place for their own clients.

Should the issuer go to the underwriter's office when all this is going on, or monitor the sale from home? Definitely the latter. There is nothing the issuer can get at the senior managing underwriter's office that he or she cannot get at his or her own desk. Austin Tobin, the negotiation and pricing adviser we met in Chapter 5, advises his clients, "To control the price negotiation, the issuer must be free from undue pressure.

"There are compelling reasons for the issuer to exercise that control from his or her offices rather than at the offices of the underwriter:

1 Home field advantage.
2 Familiar routine.
3 Preestablished and familiar lines of communication.
4 Time to examine suggested pricing changes with deliberation.
5 Ability to make decisions in an unhurried manner.
6 Maintenance of a nonconfrontational approach to the negotiation."

In short, if you want a trip to the big city, do it before the sale to meet your bankers, or at the closing.

ONE OF THE most useful documents produced after a negotiated sale is the **pricing book**. This is a book put together by the managing underwriter to show you the final structure of the issue, how it did comparable to historical and concurrent sales, who made what, and who bought what. It will all be collected here, and very clearly.

The best reading an issuer can do before gearing up for a future bond sale is to read the responses to its previous RFPs, then read the pricing book for its last sale. There is no better or more comprehensive guide to the market and its ways.

CREDIT RATINGS

THE DECISION HAS been made to sell municipal bonds. You must next decide if you are going to apply for a credit rating or attempt to sell your bonds without a rating.

Approximately one-third of the new-issue market is unrated. There are reasons not to obtain a bond rating, and fear of the awful truth ranks pretty far down the list, as these things go. Bond ratings cost money, "from $1,000 to $350,000," as Moody's Investors Service discloses on the back cover of its weekly *Credit Perspectives;* and small and infrequent (which is not to say insolvent) issuers often decide to come to market with no rating at all. Their debt is most often purchased by a local bank or an institution familiar with the credit. Judging strictly by what unrated bonds generally yield in the secondary market, unrated paper seems to trade about where A-rated paper does. Some analysts have alleged that going to market without a rating costs issuers more, but this has not been proved.

Most issuers, however, do get ratings from one, two, or even three of the credit rating agencies that serve the municipal market on a regular basis. They do so because it makes their bonds easier to sell. Most institutional investors like a bond to have at least two ratings, and some are even precluded from buying bonds unless they have two ratings.

Controversy at the Rating Agencies

LIKE MOST OF THE MUNICIPAL MARKET, the world of the rating agencies has not been untouched by controversy in recent years. In 1994, for example, Jefferson County School District No. R-1 in Colorado sued Moody's for publishing an unsolicited, and as it happens, negative rating, contending that Moody's downgrade on the day of the pricing harmed the issuer.

A federal judge later dismissed the charges, ruling that Moody's opinion was protected by the First Amendment. A look at Moody's unusually detailed "Special Comment," released after the judge ruled on the matter, illustrates how the agencies approach their job and incidentally provides a rare behind-the-scenes look into one agency's organizational thought process. We go into it at length here because the controversy over so-called unsolicited ratings is not likely to abate soon.

Moody's first responded to the charge that it had issued a rating without being requested for one:

> Moody's has maintained a rating on Jefferson County School District's General Obligation Bonds since December 1952. Over this period, we have

had regular discussions with representatives of the School District in our offices in New York and in Jefferson County. In October 1992, Moody's downgraded the School District's general obligation bonds to A from A1 due in part to Colorado's past underfunding of the School Finance Act and ongoing financial pressures on the School District.

On its next bond sale in October 1993, the School District did not apply to Moody's for a rating. The new issue of 1993 Series bonds was on a parity with the outstanding rated debt, meaning that the security for the bondholders was identical and that Moody's outstanding rating applied to the new issue. In accordance with its long-standing policy, Moody's reviewed the School District's existing general obligation debt rating, taking into consideration the new offering of debt. Even though on this occasion the School District did not request a rating, we felt that, given the passage of Amendment 1 and the uncertainties it created for bondholders, our obligation to existing and future holders of the School District's GO debt dictated that we analyze and comment on the credit quality of the 1993 Series bonds issued by the School District. Among other provisions, Amendment 1 prohibited increases in property taxes without referendum and did not distinguish between property taxes levied for operations and those levied for debt service on previously issued GO unlimited tax bonds. Many issuers knew of Moody's opinion and concern regarding Amendment 1 and were concerned that Amendment 1 could lead to a downgrading of ratings.

The rating agency then addressed the question of whether or not it had "ambushed" the issuer by somehow springing the rating on them on the day of their pricing:

Moody's learned of the scheduled $111 million offering of the 1993 Series bonds on the evening of October 19, 1993 (the day before the pricing) through a telephone inquiry from a potential investor who wanted to receive a Moody's opinion on this and many other issues coming to market. This unanticipated information placed Moody's in a difficult position on the night prior to pricing. Moody's knew that the School District had ongoing financial pressures and that there were uncertainties regarding Amendment 1. Our choice was either to announce the next day our intention to review the rating (to give investors facing an imminent purchase decision the benefit of our opinion at the time) or to remain silent and rate the transaction after closing (in which case investors who had purchased bonds without the benefit of our current opinion might be injured).

On the morning of October 20, we confirmed with the lead underwriter that the School District was indeed proceeding with a sale of parity debt and informed the School District, its underwriter and the market of our intention to rate as soon as we had an opportunity to complete our analysis. The sequence of events and our obligation to investors left us with no other responsible alternative. In our comment, we promptly informed the market that we had an existing rating on the School District's outstanding general obligation debt and that we intended to review that rating. We acted as quickly as we could, but the timing of events was determined by the School District's failure to notify us in advance of the sale. If we had known about the sale prior to the eve of pricing, we would have informed the School District and the market at that time of our intention to rate.

The school district did not want a rating; in fact, it requested that Moody's withdraw its existing ratings. "In a letter dated October 19, 1993 (the day before the pricing), the School District's representatives requested that we withdraw our existing rating on its general obligation debt," the agency wrote in its Special Comment on the matter. "That letter, because it was sent via overnight mail rather than fax, did not reach us until after the pricing had taken place and our comment had been published."

Not, however, that even a faxed letter would have mattered:

> It is very unusual for an issuer to request Moody's to withdraw a rating from the marketplace. It is even more unusual for Moody's to honor such a request. For us to do so would be tantamount to allowing issuers to suppress our rating opinions whenever they did not like our opinions or preferred others. We could envision many requests for withdrawals of ratings just prior to downgrades. For Moody's to engage in, or tolerate, such a practice would violate our commitment to provide independent and objective information to the marketplace and would convert Moody's from an independent observer of the capital formation process into a selling tool of the issuer. Ultimately, such conduct on our part would compromise the credibility of our ratings with investors and, in turn, reduce ratings' utility to issuers.

Jefferson County School District was not the only one to complain about an unsolicited rating. In 1997, the Arvada Urban Renewal Authority, which also happens to be in Jefferson County, Colorado, said an unsolicited rating on an insured refunding issue cost it more than $300,000. This marked the first time that an issuer complained specifically about the new Moody's policy of assigning underlying ratings to insured deals.

The Justice Department in 1996 said it was looking into just how much pressure the rating agencies put on issuers to get ratings in the first place, and more than one congressman has called for the outright regulation of the rating agencies. To date, there has been no result of the Justice Department probe. All attempts at regulation have died.

Issuers should keep in mind Moody's own advice in its *Guide to Ratings, Rating Practices, and Rating Process*: "The rating process does not end with the sale and closing of a municipal finance transaction. Rating currency is a critical facet of Moody's services to investors and issuers, and, therefore, the Public Finance Group regularly reviews outstanding ratings to confirm their accuracy and makes changes as needed."

Remember, too, that the rating agencies, which did not even start charging municipal issuers for ratings until the 1960s, view investors as the primary customers for their services. Standard & Poor's observed: "The value of a rating emanates from the validity of criteria and reliability of judgment and analysis of Standard & Poor's professional staff."

The Rating Process

IN ITS *Municipal Finance Criteria,* a 253-page book published annually that describes the rating process, the agency continued, "Standard & Poor's operates with no government mandate, subpoena powers, or any other official authority. As part of the media, Standard & Poor's has a right to express its opinions in the form of letter symbols. Recognition as a rating agency relies on investor's willingness to accept its judgment." And what is a rating all about? Standard & Poor's answers: "The rating performs the isolated function of credit risk evaluation, which is one element of the entire investment decision-making process."

Moody's notes that although ratings are usually assigned at the request of issuers, "if there is interest in the credit risk of a debt issue, Moody's reserves the right to assign and publish a rating without the issuer's request or permission."

Standard & Poor's, on the other hand, does not assign ratings without a request. "There's no value in me trying to guess how an issuer is," comments Vladimir Stadnyk, who runs public finance at Standard & Poor's. "Information is not easy to come by readily, quickly, and efficiently, and we need the interaction. It's not the same if you're rating by documentation only. We like to have an open relationship, and an ongoing dialogue, with issuers. We want to provide service, but provide service the most intelligent way we can."

The rating process evaluates an issuer's ability to pay and also attempts to gauge, as much as practicable, an issuer's willingness to pay. Willingness to pay usually comes to light only around election time. If voters are presented with an array of initiatives to limit taxes and the financial flexibility that comes with them, not once, but again, and again, and again, it is a pretty clear sign that there is taxpayer discontent at some level, and that one of these measures, with its slew of unintended consequences, just might pass.

What do the rating agencies look for? A lot. For all the buzz about disclosure, the municipal market still lacks what Stadnyk calls "adequate, consistent, and standardized information."

For tax-supported bonds and notes, Moody's says it typically likes to see primary documents including:
◆ Official statement.
◆ Notice of sale, for a competitive deal.
◆ Legal opinion.

◆ Annual reports or audits for the past three years.
◆ Most recent operating budget.
◆ Capital budget or planning document.
◆ Copy of the local charter or other document that describes the governmental structure.
◆ In the case of school districts, 10-year enrollment trend and projection, as well as a description of the school's facilities and capacity.

SUPPORT DOCUMENTS THE AGENCY would like to see in the case of tax-supported debt, to the extent the information is not contained in any of the above, include:

◆ Assessed valuation for the past five years.
◆ Equalization ratios for the past five years.
◆ List of the 10 largest taxpayers and their assessed valuation.
◆ Current population and latest census estimates.
◆ Tax rates and levies for the past five years, including collections of the current year's levy and total tax collections, and tax rates of overlapping jurisdictions.
◆ Tax assessment and collection procedures, including due dates and penalty rates.
◆ Tax and/or levy limitations.
◆ Debt or interest rate limits.
◆ Statement of direct debt and debt of overlapping debt issuers, including allocable share.
◆ Annual principal and interest payments of new and outstanding debt, with debt segregated by security pledge.
◆ Future plans for debt issuance.
◆ Number and dollar amount of building permits over the past five years.
◆ Number of governmental employees, whether unionized, and contract status.
◆ Statement regarding status of employee pension funds, including the latest actuarial study, if available.

◆ Local and area unemployment rates.
◆ List of 10 leading employers, including number of employees and type of business for each.
◆ Area of the issuer in square miles, and percentage developed.
◆ Investment policy: either a formal document or a brief description of practices.

ALL THIS, BEAR IN MIND, is for tax-supported, general obligation debt. But say you're not selling tax-supported debt. You're a private college or university, looking at the municipal bond market. Here is what Standard & Poor's says it requires in the way of documentation:

◆ Bond resolution or indenture.
◆ Lease or mortgage.
◆ Official statement.
◆ Five years of enrollment information broken down into undergraduates and graduates and full- and part-time status.
◆ Five years of first-time freshman application information, including acceptances, matriculants, and student quality indicators and average test scores.
◆ Top-10 competitor institutions and win/loss statistics, if available.
◆ Program offerings; program additions and deletions over the past five years.
◆ Five years of student tuition and room charges.
◆ Five years of faculty information broken down into full- and part-time faculty, percentage tenured, and percentage holding doctorates.
◆ Five years of audited financial statements.
◆ History of state appropriations and formula used to determine appropriation, if applicable.
◆ History of annual giving, capital campaign, and fund drives, including participation rates and goal success.
◆ Endowment investment and spending policy.

Steps in the Credit Rating Process

THE LOWER AN ISSUER'S credit rating, the more it will have to pay in order to borrow money. Investors who take more risk demand more reward, and more reward comes in the form of higher yield.

There are a number of ways for you to enhance your credit rating, however, and thus to lower the cost of your borrowings significantly. You can do so with bank letters of credit, bond insurance, and special state programs that provide a layer of protection to an issuer's existing credit. Some issuers have even found it cost-effective to use a state guarantee program to raise their ratings to investment grade, and then to wrap the entire transaction further, with a bond insurance policy. All this is done in the name of shaving a few extra basis points off borrowing costs, because, as we have seen, those basis points add up: 5 or 10 basis points can translate into millions of dollars of savings over the life of a transaction.

The easiest and most inexpensive programs for an issuer to use are the various "public credit enhancements" available. These include 22 various programs in 18 states, and more are being created each year. They range from simple promises of a state to withhold school aid payments (Pennsylvania and South Carolina, among others) or motor vehicle tax payments (California) to a direct guarantee of local school debt (the Texas Permanent School Fund). Such programs offer issuers a chance to get minimum ratings on their bond issues of anywhere from A-minus right up to triple-A, depending on the program and the rating agency involved. These avenues should be explored first by any issuer looking to sell debt.

Municipal bond insurance has been around since 1971, and since its inception has grown to cover nearly 50 percent of the dollar volume of bonds sold in a given year. The insurance is sold by four major players who go by their acronyms: AMBAC, FGIC, FSA, and MBIA, as well as a number of smaller ones. In return for an up-front premium, the insurer guarantees payment of principal and interest on a bond.

The insurers write to what they call "a zero-loss standard," which means that they do not expect to have to make payments on credits they insure. In other words, the insurers do not usually cover credits that are rated below investment grade. They have, however, made payments when called upon; and do, on occasion, insure financings that are below investment grade.

The insurers are highly competitive, and their premiums have declined steadily throughout the years. This means that issuers can get it, if they think it will lower their debt service costs, for as little as 10 basis points (.10 percent) of the total debt service on a bond issue, although more typical premiums range from 25 to 75 basis points or so.

Insurance provides bond buyers with "sleep insurance." Retail buyers seem to like it, and salesmen regard it as a means of simplifying their job. Rather than trying to explain the details of a particular bond issue, a salesman can just say that the issue is insured as to repayment of principal and interest. The only grumblers at the party thus far have been

(continued on following page)

institutional investors and fund managers, who don't mind doing the extra research on a transaction in return for a little extra yield. These parties contend that the insurers have sucked the value out of the market and made bond issues much more of a commodity product, and not coincidentally have made their jobs, which is to maximize return for their shareholders, that much harder.

The job for the issuer is to ensure that the use of insurance is actually economically justifiable. At least one issuer already rated a natural triple-A, the Alaska Housing Finance Corp., has used insurance to enhance its market reception. On the other side of the coin, at least one issuer rated a high double-A, Wisconsin, actually prohibited underwriters from bidding on its deal if they were going to do so using insurance, because, in the words of capital finance director Frank Hoadley, insurance "cheapens the credit" in the secondary market.

Finally, a new insurer was founded late last year, to guarantee what it called the "underserved" sections of the municipal market—the unrated, or below investment grade market. Called American Capital Access, the firm expected that it would be able to take such credits and insure them to its own double-A level, thus saving the issuers anywhere from 35 to 65 basis points, depending on maturity. The company expects to insure about $4 billion of the estimated $25 billion or so of unrated deals that come to market each year.

◆ Capital improvement and future debt plans.
◆ Brief management biographies.
◆ Description of governing board or body and relationship with institution.

THE CHART ON the following two pages details the steps of the credit-rating process, as described in Standard & Poor's *Municipal Finance Criteria*. The process is similar at the other rating agencies. After the documentation is submitted, the issuer either visits the rating agency, or the rating agency's analysts perform an on-site inspection. The decision is usually driven in part by the financial adviser, and in part by the actual project—it may not be necessary for analysts to visit or revisit a city, but it most likely will be if the subject financing is for a project. An in-house visit to a rating agency generally takes a few hours. A site visit will likely take most of a day.

Finally, once the decision has been made and you learn your rating, there is always the possibility of appeal. Moody's observes:

> At times during the preparation of an initial rating, it becomes apparent that the rating will not reach the level expected or sought by the party requesting the rating.
>
> It is always Moody's intent that the rating process be clear to issuers and that our judgments be sound and fair. We therefore strive to ensure that issues and their intermediaries are made aware at an early stage in the analytic process of all issues that may ultimately affect the outcome of the rating decision. Dialogue through each step of the rating process is intended to provide issuers with an adequate opportunity to respond to our concerns so that they are not surprised by the rating eventually assigned.

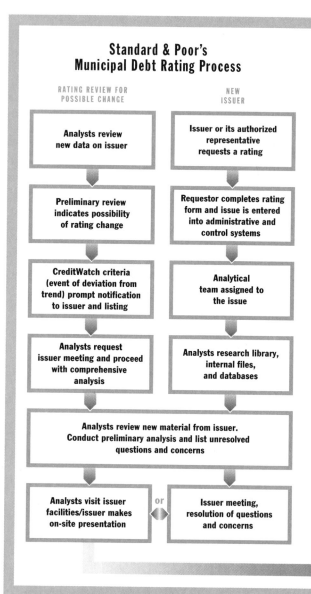

Standard & Poor's Municipal Debt Rating Process

RATING REVIEW FOR POSSIBLE CHANGE	NEW ISSUER
Analysts review new data on issuer	Issuer or its authorized representative requests a rating
Preliminary review indicates possibility of rating change	Requestor completes rating form and issue is entered into administrative and control systems
CreditWatch criteria (event of deviation from trend) prompt notification to issuer and listing	Analytical team assigned to the issue
Analysts request issuer meeting and proceed with comprehensive analysis	Analysts research library, internal files, and databases

Analysts review new material from issuer. Conduct preliminary analysis and list unresolved questions and concerns

Analysts visit issuer facilities/issuer makes on-site presentation	or	Issuer meeting, resolution of questions and concerns

Final analytical review preparation
of rating profile and
committee presentation

Presentation of the analysis to rating
committee/Discussion and vote to
determine rating

Notification of rating
decision to issuer or its
authorized representative

Does issuer wish to appeal
by furnishing additional
information?

yes — no

**Presentation
of additional
information to rating
committee/Discussion
and vote to confirm
or modify rating**

**Formal notification
to issuer or
its authorized
representative.
Rating is released**

Rating entered into
Standard & Poor's rating
surveillance system

SOURCE: STANDARD & POOR'S

Nevertheless, occasions may arise where fundamental disagreement exists between the issuer and Moody's over the rating conclusion that has been reached. On such occasions it is possible for an issuer to appeal the rating prior to its public release. In those instances where an issuer can provide material new information that they believe was not properly weighed, a review of the rating will be undertaken. The views of the issuer and the new information will be reviewed by Moody's analysts and rating committee members, and a final rating decision will be made.

Standard & Poor's has a similar process, but, as Vladimir Stadnyk pointed out, "the appeal is not designed to argue key points. There are two things brought up at an appeal: clarification, or new and previously unavailable information. Since we have a constant dialogue with issuers, we like to think that we don't blindside them." Of perhaps a dozen or so appeals made in 1996, he estimated that one was actually successful.

AFTER THE SALE

12

YOU'VE SOLD YOUR bond issue. Congratulations! But navigating the primary-market minefield is only the first step. Putting it to good use is the final step; reinvestment of proceeds is how you get there.

Reinvestment Strategy

AS A PUBLIC ENTITY with expensive borrowed funds, the issuer has the following goals:

◆ Maximizing return on investment.

◆ Ensuring that funds are available when needed.

◆ Minimizing investment risk.

◆ Minimizing administrative expenditures.

◆ Avoiding unexpected transfers to private

parties, that is, yield-burning.

Unfortunately, several of these goals may conflict. To develop an appropriate investment strategy requires answering a few questions.

1 What is the money needed for? How definite is the payout schedule? Construction funds with a fairly predictable payout schedule are different from emergency funds, which by their nature are unpredictable, and from debt service funds, where the payout schedule is defined up front and will not deviate.

2 Are available triple-A investment rates higher or lower than your borrowing cost? If the answer is higher, then you have room to buy securities with the lowest risk and lowest administrative cost, knowing that the excess yield will be absorbed by the federal government. If the answer is lower, now you have all the tradeoffs noted above.

3 Does your state offer a state-managed or state-sponsored money market fund? If the answer is yes, then construction fund money should go there.

In general, if there is a fixed payout schedule, you should buy securities whose income stream matches that schedule. For a refunding escrow, if special state and local government series Treasury securities (SLGS) work, then buy SLGS. If the yield on SLGS is too low (below the borrowing cost), then buy a fixed portfolio of U.S. Treasury securities on the open market. Have the financial adviser determine which portfolio is appropriate, then run a competitive bid to buy them. Each security, meaning each maturity, should be bid on and awarded separately. The financial adviser should not be allowed to bid on the securities. Only in this manner will the issuer get the best price, get the highest yield, and avoid making an unexpected transfer of wealth to the provider of the investments.

By contrast, to the extent that there is an unknown payout schedule and the amount to be invested is more than $10 million, that portion of the investments should be placed into a **guaranteed investment contract (GIC)** with a fixed rate of return, the right to withdraw funds as projected, and the right to postpone withdrawals while preserving the investment rate.

Such a contract can be obtained by competitive bid from among a variety of AA-rated institutions and can be structured to be rated triple-A, if necessary. Competitive bidding will produce the highest rate. There is no need for an investment broker. Your senior managing underwriter or financial adviser will conduct the bidding for you with no added charge above their management or advisory fee. Insist that no broker's commission is to be paid. Further insist that neither your senior managing underwriter nor your financial adviser be allowed to bid on the securities if they are also the ones running the bid. Make sure that you see and approve the final bid form and that the actual bids are received at your office, not the banker's or financial adviser's. (This simple step eliminates most of the risk of hidden fees or rigged bids.)

These two guidelines are not all or nothing. To the extent that the payout schedule can be determined, use the fixed portfolio approach with the guaranteed investment contract filling in the gaps. Thus, for a refunding escrow, all of the dates are known and the portfolio approach is the way to go. For a construction fund, one might use a portion of each. For a reserve fund, in which withdrawals are unlikely but must be available if necessary, the GIC approach works best.

RESOURCES

MUNICIPAL FINANCE OFFICERS can read about their bond market on a minute-by-minute basis, if they desire, and if they subscribe to the news wire services produced by Bloomberg, Dow Jones, Reuters, or Thomson. These can cost from several hundred to several thousand dollars per month, however, and are probably a little more than all but the most frequent issuers can use.

The market is also served by one daily newspaper, *The Bond Buyer,* published since 1891 and owned by Thomson Financial Publishing. The cover price is $1,897 per year, although issuer discounts are available. It is chock-full of useful statistical information and news articles and has an especially good Washington bureau. Once again, however, this is probably more than the casual or occasional issuer really needs.

The Bond Buyer also puts out an annual statistical yearbook, which includes information on volume, interest rates, underwriters, credit enhancement, investors, and various sector highlights. The yearbook is $95. *The Bond Buyer,* One State Street Plaza, New York, NY 10004 (212-803-8200).

Finally, *The Bond Buyer* publishes a telephone directory listing just about everyone you need to sell your bond issue. *The Bond Buyer's Municipal Marketplace,* or *Red Book,* has been published since the 1930s. It has spring and fall editions, and costs $400. It is available from Thomson Financial Publishing (847-676-9600).

The Blue List is a daily publication owned by Standard & Poor's, so-called because of the blue paper on which it is printed. It was once referred to as a "municipal bond novel" by a trader some years back, a characterization that still rings true. Here is what is trading in the market, and how much it costs. It is conveniently organized by state and also features separate listings for zero-coupon bonds, bank-qualified bonds, bonds subject to the alternative minimum tax, taxable bonds, and industrial development bonds backed by corporations, among others.

A subscription to the *Blue List* costs $850 in the Wall Street area, and $1,050 out of town. This is also probably a little more than you want to spend if you are responsible for one or two small bond sales per year.

The Government Finance Officers Association (GFOA) is based in Chicago and has 14,000 members; $30 of each member's dues is earmarked for the organization's useful bimonthly magazine, *Government Finance Review.* The organization also puts out a number of short, easily accessible, straight-English booklets about borrowing in the municipal market. These include:

◆ *Pricing Bonds in a Negotiated Sale: How to Manage the Process* (1994; 30 pages, $5).

◆ *Competitive v. Negotiated: How to Choose the Method of Sale for Tax-Exempt Bonds* (1994; 14 pages, $5).

◆ *Structuring and Sizing the Bond Issue: How to Develop an Optimal Approach* (1995; 34 pages, $9).

◆ *Purchasing Credit Enhancement: How to Decide if Bond Insurance Makes Sense* (1994; 15 pages, $5).

◆ *Debt Issuance and Management: A Guide for Smaller Governments* (1994; 136 pages, $18).

Government Finance Review is aimed at a fairly sophisticated reader and contains articles by both academics and practitioners of public finance; the booklets are aimed at the beginner. The GFOA can be reached at 312-977-9700.

Grant's puts out two publications dealing with the municipal bond market. *Grant's Municipal Bond Issuer* is a fortnightly magazine devoted to public finance in general and the municipal market in particular; it is available to qualified issuers for free. Everyone else—financial advisers, traders, salesmen, insurers, analysts—can subscribe at a cost of $500 per year.

Grant's also puts out a fortnightly called *Grant's Municipal Bond Observer,* which is primarily aimed at the trade and the sophisticated buyer. It is available for $645. Grant's can be reached at 212-809-7994.

MBIA, the bond insurer, puts out a quarterly publication called *Public Issues,* which uses the GFOA's mailing list. Its articles are more general and anecdotal than *Government Finance Review*'s. The editor, Jude Westerfield, can be reached at 914-765-3887.

Another resource to take a look at is the *Municipal Finance Journal.* This quarterly publication is devoted to legal, economic, and political aspects of municipal finance. The editor, Dr. W. Bartley Hildreth, can be reached at 316-978-6332.

A small number of newsletters cover the market, although most of them are aimed strictly at either the investor, the analyst, or the trade.

Dennis Walters, who for many years ran *The Bond Buyer*'s Los Angeles bureau, now publishes *The Cal-Bond Journal,* a fortnightly dedicated to "Shedding Light on California's Public Finance Field," which can certainly use it. The subscription rate is $299. Walters can be reached at 805-640-3436.

Both Moody's and Standard & Poor's publish weekly magazines containing feature articles done by their analysts, as well as rating news. Moody's *Credit Perspec-*

tives costs $1,500 a year (800-811-6980). Standard & Poor's *CreditWeek Municipal* is $2,475 annually (212-208-1146). Fitch Investors Service provides all of its research for free on the Internet.

Most books on public finance and the municipal market are at least badly dated, when they are not out of print altogether. One of the better ones is Robert Zipf's *How Municipal Bonds Work* (1995; New York Institute of Finance; 260 pages, $15.95). The same publisher put out an 878-page *Handbook of Municipal Bonds and Public Finance,* edited by Robert Lamb, James Leigland, and Stephen Rappaport (1993) for $90.

Seattle-Northwest Securities Corp. published *An Introduction to Tax-Exempt Financing for Indian Tribes,* by one of their bankers, Jesse M. Smith. The book is crisply written and packs a lot into its 121 pages, and it is the primary sourcebook for this specialized area of finance. The author can be reached in the Portland office, at 503-275-8307.

Databases

DELPHIS HANOVER CORP., located in Southbury, Connecticut (203-262-1862) has recorded bond issues sales since 1963. Each maturity of these bond issues is evaluated both as to relative market price and basis point relationship to its bond rating.

Thomson-owned Securities Data Co. (SDC) tracks municipal bond sales and securities firms. SDC, which is located in Newark, New Jersey (973-622-3100), can provide you with reams of information about bond volume, sales by sector, and which underwriters, financial advisers, and bond counsel are leaders in their respective sectors, states, or regions.

Web Sites

THE INTERNET HAS lots of information on municipal bonds. Unfortunately, most of it is aimed at investors in municipal bonds, not issuers of them. There is very little good, practical, uninterested advice on public finance available.

If you are looking for current stories regarding the municipal bond market, you can go to **www.bondbuyer.com**, which will take you to the latest index of *Bond Buyer* stories that are available on the Internet.

For a look at what larger issuers think is important, surf around and take a look at their sites.

Associations

THE MOST IMPORTANT association for the new municipal issuer to join is the Government Finance Officers Association (GFOA), which is based in Chicago and has more than 14,000 members. The GFOA's base membership fees range from $120 for officials from cities and counties with populations of less than 5,000, up to $3,645 for those from cities and counties with more than 1 million in population; additional memberships are $115. The GFOA can be reached at 312-977-9700. The executive director is Jeffrey L. Esser.

The Council of State Governments and the National Association of State Treasurers (NAST) are located in Lexington, Kentucky. The number is 606-244-8175. NAST, in turn, helps organize the State Debt Management Network, which holds a number of educational programs throughout the year.

Regulators

PAUL MACO HEADS the SEC's Office of Municipal Securities (202-942-7305).

Christopher Taylor is executive director of the Municipal Securities Rulemaking Board (202-223-9347).

GLOSSARY

Acceleration A provision, normally present in a bond indenture agreement, mortgage, or other contract, that the unpaid balance is to become due and payable if specified events of default should occur. These include failure to meet interest, principal, or sinking fund payments; insolvency; and nonpayment of taxes on mortgaged property.

Acquired purpose obligations A term used in IRS regulations to describe loans taken out to meet a municipality's governmental obligations.

Ad valorem tax A tax based on the value of property.

Additional bonds test A legal requirement that new additional bonds, which will have a claim to revenues already pledged to outstanding revenue bonds, can be issued only if certain financial or other requirements are met.

Advance refunding A method of providing for payment of debt service on a municipal bond until the first call date or maturity from funds other than an issuer's revenues. Advance refundings are done by selling a new bond issue and investing the proceeds in a portfolio of U.S. government securities structured in order to provide enough cash flow to pay debt service on the refunded bonds. The old issue is then considered to be advance refunded.

Agreement among underwriters The contract set up between members of an underwriting syndicate, stipulating the activities of each member.

Amortization The elimination of debt through scheduled payments.

Any interest date call A call feature under which an issuer can redeem outstanding securities on any interest payment date, after the first call date.

Appropriations An authorization by a legislative body to set aside cash for a specific purpose. Certificates of participation, for example, are backed by appropriations—unlike general obligations bonds, which are backed by a municipality's taxing power, or revenue bonds, which are backed by specified revenues.

Arbitrage The practice of simultaneously buying and selling an item in different markets to profit from a spread in prices or yields resulting from market conditions. Municipal issuers, except under certain circumstances, are prohibited from making arbitrage profits, i.e., from selling tax-exempt bonds and investing them in higher-yielding taxable obligations in order to earn profits. Such profits must be rebated to the Treasury.

Artifice or device A term used in section 103 of the IRS code to describe a transaction that enables the issuer to gain arbitrage profits.

Authority A unit or agency of a municipality established to perform a single function or group of functions, usually supported by user fees.

Authorization ordinance A law that allows a municipality to sell a specific bond issue or finance a specific project.

Average effective interest cost The average interest rate on a bond issue, including all issuance costs, expressed as either net interest cost or true interest cost.

Average life The average length of time an issue of bonds with mandatory sinking funds is expected to remain outstanding.

Baby bond (1) A denomination issued in less than $1,000, also known as a mini-bond; rarely used. (2) A bond issued by the State of Louisiana during Reconstruction, featuring the picture of a baby on its face.

Balloon maturity An extremely large proportion of bond principal coming due in a single year.

Bank qualified Bonds issued by municipalities that are certain they will sell $10 million or less in bonds per year. Certain financial institutions that buy these securities are allowed to deduct 80 percent of the interest expense incurred to buy them.

Basis point One one-hundredth of a point. One hundred basis points equal 1 percent. Used in discussing the pricing and yields of bond issues.

Bid The price offered by prospective purchasers of securities.

Bid wanted A listing of securities put out by a dealer asking for bids on part or all of them.

Black-box deal Term to describe a variety of abusive

bond issues sold in the 1980s in which the proceeds were used to earn arbitrage profits and nothing more.

Blind pool A bond issue sold without the specific borrowers or projects they wish to finance known in advance.

Block A large amount of bonds trading in the market, generally speaking, $100,000 or more.

Blue List A daily publication by Standard & Poor's, printed on distinctive blue paper, showing what dealers are offering for sale from their inventory in the so-called secondary market. The *Blue List* volume is the total par value of all bonds offered for sale in the publication, properly entitled *The Blue List of Current Municipal and Corporate Offerings.*

Blue Sky law A term referring to various state laws enacted to protect the public against securities fraud.

Boilerplate Commonly repeated legal sections of an official statement, which vary little from transaction to transaction.

Bond A representation by a government or corporation that it will repay a loan, with interest either stated or, in the case of zero-coupon bonds, imputed. Most bonds today are sold in paperless, electronic format. Municipal bonds generally mature in 12 months or more. Securities with shorter maturities are termed notes, or commercial paper.

Bond anticipation note A short-term borrowing that is retired with the proceeds of a bond sale.

Bond banks State bond banks buy loans from localities and bundle them into larger offerings, affording small issuers certain advantages of scale.

Bond Buyer, The The daily, and only, newspaper of record of the municipal market, published since 1891. The paper was known first as *The Daily Bond Buyer* and changed its name to the current one in 1987.

Bond Buyer Index Generally used in reference to *The Bond Buyer* 20-bond general obligation (GO) bond index, which is calculated weekly using 20 GO bonds maturing in 20 years. The index has a rating roughly equivalent to a double-A. Eleven of the same bonds are also used to calculate an index equivalent to a double-A-plus.

The 20- and 11-bond indexes were compiled monthly from 1917 to 1946; they are now compiled weekly. The record high for the 20-bond index was 13.44 percent, which it hit on January 14, 1982. The record low was 1.29 percent, which it posted on February 14, 1946. The record high for the 11-bond index was 13.05 percent; the record low was 1.04 percent.

The Bond Buyer started a weekly revenue bond index in 1979, comprising 25 revenue bonds maturing in 30 years, with an average rating of A-plus. Its high was 14.32 percent, also reached in January 1982.

In 1989 the newspaper also started a short-term tax-exempt note index calculated using 10 various note issuers.

The bond issuers used in the calculation of all of the indexes change from time to time, as their fortunes rise or fall.

Bond Buyer Municipal Bond Index An index of bond prices designed by the Chicago Board of Trade used in trading municipal bond futures, and sometimes used by observers as a benchmark in assessing the state of the municipal market.

Bond contract Terms of the agreement between issuer and buyer, typically including the bond resolution, trust indenture, and various security provisions.

Bond counsel A lawyer who reviews the transaction and writes an opinion on its legality, security, and tax status.

Bond election The process by which voters approve or reject the sale of general obligation (G0) bonds, held throughout the year, depending on locality.

Bond fund A portfolio of municipal bonds that offers shares to investors either through closed-end funds or unit investment trusts, which offer shares of fixed portfolios of municipal bonds; or through open-ended, managed, or mutual funds, which offer shares in actively managed portfolios of same.

Bond insurance Insurance purchased by an issuer or an underwriter for all or part of a bond issue, which guarantees principal and interest payments, as due. Such insurance results in a higher credit rating, lower borrowing cost, or enhanced marketability for the bonds thus insured.

Bond purchase agreement The contract between the issuer and the underwriter setting the terms, prices, and conditions of the sale.

Bond ratings The series of letters, numbers, and symbols used by rating agencies to designate the credit quality of an issuer's securities.

Bond register A record, kept by a transfer agent or registrar on behalf of an issuer, of the names and addresses of registered bond owners.

Bond resolution A legal document describing the terms and conditions of the offering, the rights of the bondholder, and the obligations of the issuer. Also known as the indenture of trust.

Bond transcript The legal documents associated with a bond offering.

Bond year $1,000 of debt outstanding for one year. The number of bond years in an issue is the number of bonds times the number of years from the dated date to maturity. The number of bond years is used in calculating the average life of an issue and its net interest cost.

Bonded debt The portion of an issuer's total indebtedness as represented by outstanding bonds.
◆ *Direct or gross bonded debt:* The sum of the total bonded debt and short-term debt.
◆ *Net direct debt or bonded debt:* Direct debt less sinking fund accumulations and all self-supporting debt.
◆ *Total overall debt or total direct and overlapping debt:* Total direct debt plus the issuer's applicable share of the total debt of all overlapping jurisdictions.
◆ *Net overall debt or net direct and overlapping debt:* Net direct debt plus the issuer's applicable share of the total debt of all overlapping jurisdictions.
◆ *Overlapping debt:* The issuer's share of the debt of other local units.

Book Presale orders for a new bond issue, based on preliminary price levels. The syndicate member who keeps track of orders is said to be the senior book-running manager.

Book entry Securities in the form of entries in the issuer's or a clearing house's books, rather than in the form of paper certificates with coupons. All but the smallest bond issues are sold in book-entry format.

Broker An agent between buyers and sellers of securities. Brokers' brokers handle interdealer transactions.

Calendar The list of upcoming bond sales. Bloomberg keeps an electronic version at CDRN for negotiated sales and CDRC for competitive sales.

Call Redemption of a bond prior to maturity. The first call is usually 10 years away, at par, although most issuers allow for earlier calls at a premium of 101 or 102.

Canadian interest cost (CIC) A method of calculating the interest cost, as a percentage, of a bond issue. Not used as often as the net interest cost (NIC) method.

Capital appreciation bond A bond purchased at a deep discount to face value, which pays principal and all interest at maturity.

Closing The point in the sale at which an issuer delivers securities to the underwriters, and receives the proceeds.

Competitive sale The sale of bonds through sealed bid.

Conduit financing The sale of bonds or notes for the benefit of a third party, usually a corporation.

Coupon The rate of interest to be paid by the issuer. Formerly, coupons were attached to bond certificates. They would be clipped and brought to a bank or other agent for payment.

Covenant A legally binding commitment by the issuer to the bondholder.

Cover bid The second-best bid received at a competitive sale.

Coverage The number of times project revenues are estimated to cover debt service during a 12-month period.

Dated date The date from which interest on a bond will accrue, usually the issue date.

Debt per capita Bonded debt divided by population.

Debt service reserve fund Used in revenue bond issues: a fund usually amounting to principal and interest payments for one year and used only if normal revenues do not cover debt service.

Default Failure to make timely payment of principal and interest, or to comply with other features of the indenture.

Defeasance In essence, wiping bonded indebtedness off an issuer's books through creation of a portfolio of Treasury securities sufficient to make all debt service payments on prerefunded, outstanding bonds.

Denomination The face or par amount that the issuer promises to pay at a specific bond or note maturity.

Depository A business that provides immobilization, safekeeping, and book-entry settlement services to its customers.

Designated order When a buyer gives credit to a certain dealer or dealers in an underwriting group.

Direct debt The debt that a municipality incurs in its own name.

Dollar bonds Bonds that are quoted in terms of price rather than yield. These are the biggest and most common issues in the market and trade relatively frequently.

Double-barreled bond A bond with two distinct, pledged sources of revenue.

Downgrade A reduction in an issuer's credit rating.

Due diligence The investigation of a bond issue, by underwriter's and issuer's counsel, to ensure that all material facts related to the issue have been disclosed to potential buyers in the official statement (OS).

Duration The sum of the present values of each of the principal and interest payments of a security, weighted by the time to receipt of each payment, divided by the total of the present values of the payments. Unlike average life or average maturity, duration takes into account the timing of both principal and interest payments.

Dutch auction An auction at which investors stipulate the lowest rate they will accept, usually done in conjunction with short-term securities.

Escrow account A fund set up used to pay debt service.

Face amount Par value of a bond.

Feasibility study A report by an independent expert on the economic need and practicality of a proposed program.

Financial adviser (FA) Advises issuer on matters pertaining to a proposed transaction.

Fiscal year A 12-month period not necessarily corresponding to the calendar year.

Floater A security sold with a variable rate that changes at intervals ranging from daily to annually.

Flow of funds The process stipulated in bond documents for collection and disbursal of pledged revenues.

Full faith and credit The pledge of a government's general taxing power to pay off its debt obligations.

General obligation (GO) A security backed by the full faith and credit of a municipality.

Global certificate A single certificate representing an entire issue, kept at a depository or book-entry agent.

Good faith deposit A sum of money, usually 2 percent of par value, given by bidders to issuers when they bid for competitive deals. The sum, usually given as a cashier's or certified check, is returned to the bidder if the bid is rejected.

Grant anticipation note Short-term debt that is secured by grant money expected to be received after the debt is issued.

Gross revenues Revenues of an issuer prior to the payment of expenses for operation, maintenance, and debt service.

Group net order An order confirmed to the buyer where the sales credits benefit all members of the underwriting group.

Guaranteed investment contract (GIC) In a GIC, a financial institution provides an issuer with a guaranteed rate of return.

High-grade bonds Top-rated bonds, usually triple-A.

Hospital revenue bonds Bonds sold by a state or local agency to finance construction of a hospital or nursing home, which is then operated under lease by a corporation.

Housing bonds Bonds issued by a state or local agency to finance construction of housing, and secured by mortgages. There are two types: single-family bonds, sold to provide residential mortgages, and multi-family, bonds sold to construct apartment buildings.

Indenture Legal document describing the terms and conditions of a bond offering, the rights of the bondholder, and the obligations of the issuer to the bondholder. The document is alternatively referred to as a bond resolution or deed of trust.

Industrial development bond (IDB) Also known as industrial revenue bond. IDBs are tax-exempt securities sold by a public agency to finance qualifying facilities for private enterprises, such as water and air pollution control, ports, airports, resource recovery plants, and housing. The bonds are usually repaid by revenues from the corporate beneficiary.

Interest rate swap An agreement between two parties to exchange future flows of interest payments. One party agrees to pay the other a fixed rate; the other pays the first party an adjustable rate usually tied to a short-term index. Used with some municipal bond transactions.

Inverted yield curve When short-term interest rates are higher than long-term rates.

Investment grade Designation given by a rating agency to a security in one of its top four categories, ranging from triple-A to BBB and Baa.

Joint and several obligation A form of contract in which each of the signers is obligated for the full contract amount if other signers should default.

Junior lien bonds Bond with a subordinate claim against pledged revenues.

Junk bonds Bonds rated lower than Baa by Moody's and BBB by Standard & Poor's.

Lease financings Under this structure, a municipality borrows money to rent equipment that it will acquire at the end of a stipulated period.

Legal opinion The written conclusion of a lawyer about a bond's security, legality, and tax status.

Letter of credit A form of security for many municipal bond issues, under which a bank guarantees payment of debt service under certain conditions.

Level debt service A plan under which principal and interest payments are designed to be equal over the life of a loan.

Liability Debt or other obligations.

Limited tax bonds A general obligation bond that is secured by the pledge of a specific tax or taxes.

Managers The chief members of an underwriting syndicate. The senior or book-running manager handles both the administration and allotment of the transaction.

Mandatory redemption account An account in the sinking fund into which an issuer deposits funds to be used to retire bonds as they are called.

Mark to market Taking the actual, market value of a portfolio of securities.

Market maker A bank or underwriting firm that stands ready at any time to make a bid or an offer on a security.

Maturity The date on which the principal amount of a security is due and payable.

Moral obligation bond A municipal bond that is not backed by the full faith and credit of an issuer. The issuer has no legally enforceable obligation to pay.

Net interest cost (NIC) Represents the average coupon rate of a bond issue, weighted to reflect the term and adjusted for the premium or discount. It does not consider the time value of money, as does true interest cost (TIC) or Canadian interest cost (CIC). The formula for its calculation is:

NIC = total coupon interest + discount or – premium/bond years

Net revenues Gross revenues less operating and maintenance expenses. Net revenues are divided by debt service to obtain the debt service ratio.

Notes Short-term borrowings by issuers, usually maturing in less than one year. Used to cover seasonal cash flow needs or interim financing.

Official statement (OS) A document containing detailed information about a bond issue.

Original issue discount (OID) The discount from par at which a new issue comes to market. The capital gain represented by the OID is deemed tax-exempt by the IRS.

Overlapping debt The proportionate share of debt in addition to a community's own direct obligations, such as those issued by a county or school district in which it is located.

Parity bonds Separate bond issues that have the same lien against pledged revenues.

Paying agent A bank or trust company appointed by an issuer to make principal and interest payments to bondholders.

Pay-as-you-go basis The financial policy of a municipality that finances all capital outlays from current revenues rather than borrowing.

Pledged revenues Money promised to be set aside for the payment of debt service and other deposits as required by the bond contract.

Point One percent of par value. Because bond prices are quoted as a percentage of $1,000, a point is worth $10, regardless of the actual denomination of the security.

Preliminary official statement (POS) A draft of the document containing details about a new bond issue, which does not yet contain pricing, yield, or maturity information. Often called a "red herring," because of the disclaimer, printed in red ink, prominently displayed along the edge of the cover, stating that orders may not be taken based on the document. The POS nevertheless is often used by analysts and buyers to assess credit.

Premium bond A bond whose price is above par.

Present value The current value of a cash payment to be received in the future, allowing that an amount received today could be invested for the period to the future date.

Principal The par value or face amount of a bond.

Private placement An original issue of bonds sold directly to an investor.

Rate covenant A bond indenture provision requiring rate charges necessary to meet annual debt service payments.

Ratings Credit quality evaluation of bonds and notes made by independent rating services.

Red Book Formally known as *The Bond Buyer's Municipal Marketplace,* this is the standard directory of underwriters, bond counsel, financial advisers, rating agencies, credit enhancement firms, and providers of derivatives and investment products.

Redemption Also known as a call. The exchange of cash for outstanding bonds before their maturity.

Refunding Selling a new bond issue for redemption or defeasance of an outstanding bond issue.

Sinking fund A fund established in a bond indenture that contains money available to call bonds prior to maturity.

Syndicate A group of investment banks that join to bid on a new bond issue.

Tax exempt note rate (TENR) Bankers Trust's weekly TENR is frequently used to peg the rates on variable rate bonds.

Tax increment bond Bonds whose repayment is secured by special assessments on landowners whose property stands to benefit from development or redevelopment.

True interest cost (TIC) A method of calculating interest cost while taking into account the time value of money.

Variable rate A tax-exempt security whose interest rate is reset periodically according to a preset formula. Also known as a "floater."

Visible supply The total dollar value of bonds expected to be offered over the next 30 days. A number of organizations attempt to calculate the figure, which fluctuates as issuers decide whether or not to come to market.

Warrant A certificate giving the holder the right to purchase a bond at a specific price during a certain time period.

Yield to maturity Total return on a bond, taking into consideration its coupon, length of maturity, and dollar price.

Zero-coupon bonds Bonds sold at a deep discount, and without a coupon, appreciating to full value at maturity. Also known as capital appreciation bonds.

INDEX

About Bloomberg

Bloomberg Financial Markets is a global, multi-media-based distributor of information services, combining news, data, and analysis for financial markets and businesses. Bloomberg carries real-time pricing, data, history, analytics, and electronic communications that are available 24 hours a day and are currently accessed by 250,000 financial professionals in 94 countries.

Bloomberg covers all key global securities markets, including equities, money markets, currencies, municipals, corporate/euro/sovereign bonds, commodities, mortgage-backed securities, derivative products, and governments. The company also delivers access to Bloomberg News, whose more than 540 reporters and editors in 80 bureaus worldwide provide around-the-clock coverage of economic, financial, and political events.

To learn more about Bloomberg—one of the world's fastest-growing real-time financial information networks—call a sales representative at:

Frankfurt:	49-69-920-410
Hong Kong:	852-2977-6000
London:	44-171-330-7500
New York:	1-212-318-2000
Princeton:	1-609-279-3000
San Francisco:	1-415-912-2960
São Paulo:	5511-3048-4500
Singapore:	65-226-3000
Sydney:	61-29-777-8666
Tokyo:	81-3-3201-8900

About the Author

Joe Mysak is editor of both *Grant's Municipal Bond Observer*, a fortnightly aimed at the trade and launched in July 1994, and *Grant's Municipal Bond Issuer*, a fortnightly targeted to issuers, first published in November 1997. From 1981 to March 1994, he worked at *The Bond Buyer*, as a copyeditor, reporter, assistant managing editor, managing editor, editor, and finally editor and publisher. He also served a six-month stint in 1993 as editor of *American Banker*, a sister publication of *The Bond Buyer*.

He wrote *The Guidebook to Municipal Bonds* with George J. Marlin (1992) and edited *The Bond Buyer's* centennial edition. He also cowrote *Perpetual Motion: The Illustrated History of the Port Authority of New York and New Jersey* with Judith Schiffer.